Teens, wheels, and T-shirts: an American trilogy. Photograph by Cornell Capa, circa 1957.

Summer in the city. East 110th Street. Harlem. Photograph by Raymond Depardon, 1981.

the white T
Alice Harris

Introduction by
Giorgio Armani

Designed by
Bill Anton | Service Station

Produced by
Catherine Chermayeff and
Nan Richardson | Umbra Editions

Published by
HarperStyle | An Imprint of
HarperCollins Publishers

The fantasy theater of Cirque de Soleil acrobats. Photograph by Herb Ritts, Los Angeles, 1989.

For information, write
HarperCollins*Publishers*, Inc. 10 East 53rd Street,
New York, NY 10022.

Produced by Umbra Editions, Inc.

Edited by Catherine Chermayeff,
Kathy McCarver Mnuchin, and Nan Richardson
Consulting Editor: Lala Herrero Salas
Copy Editor: Elaine Luthy

Designed by Bill Anton | Service Station Design to Inform and Promote, Inc.

Front and back jacket photo ©1996 by Harry Benson

Poster photography by Rhonda Lindle

First Edition

Umbra Editions, Inc.
180 Varick Street, New York, NY 10014

Printed in China by Palace Press International

Library of Congress Cataloging-in-Publication Data
Harris, Alice.
    the white T / edited by Catherine Chermayeff and Nan Richardson. — 1st ed.
        p.   cm.
    ISBN 0-06-270166-5
    1. T-shirt – History.   2. T-shirt – Social aspects.
    I. Title.   II. Chermayeff, Catherine.   III. Richardson, Nan.
GT2073.H37   1996
391 – dc20   96-27010
                                           CIP

HarperStyle

An Imprint of HarperCollinsPublishers
http://www.harpercollins.com

I committed myself to AIDS awareness over ten years ago when friends who had so influenced my life in profound ways started to die.

I found my voice at GMHC. It is there that we are able to give dignity and honor to all of the men, women, and children living with HIV and AIDS.

This book is dedicated to all of them.

— A. H.

A Sailor's Tale:
Origins of the T-Shirt

Stripped and ready for action at a U.S. Navy base. Brazil, circa 1945.

Fried onions and organ music at an Italian street fair. Photograph by Bruce Davidson, New York, circa 1959.

Brando, Dean, and Springsteen:
The T-Shirt in Music and Cinema

The Method, the Muscles, the Man: early Marlon Brando. Photograph by John Engstead, 1951.

Sex and Sports:
The T-Shirt Gets Physical

Days at sea. *Untitled*. Photograph by Ralph Gibson, 1974.

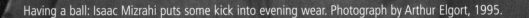

Having a ball: Isaac Mizrahi puts some kick into evening wear. Photograph by Arthur Elgort, 1995.

Best Western, painting by Eric Fischl, 1983.

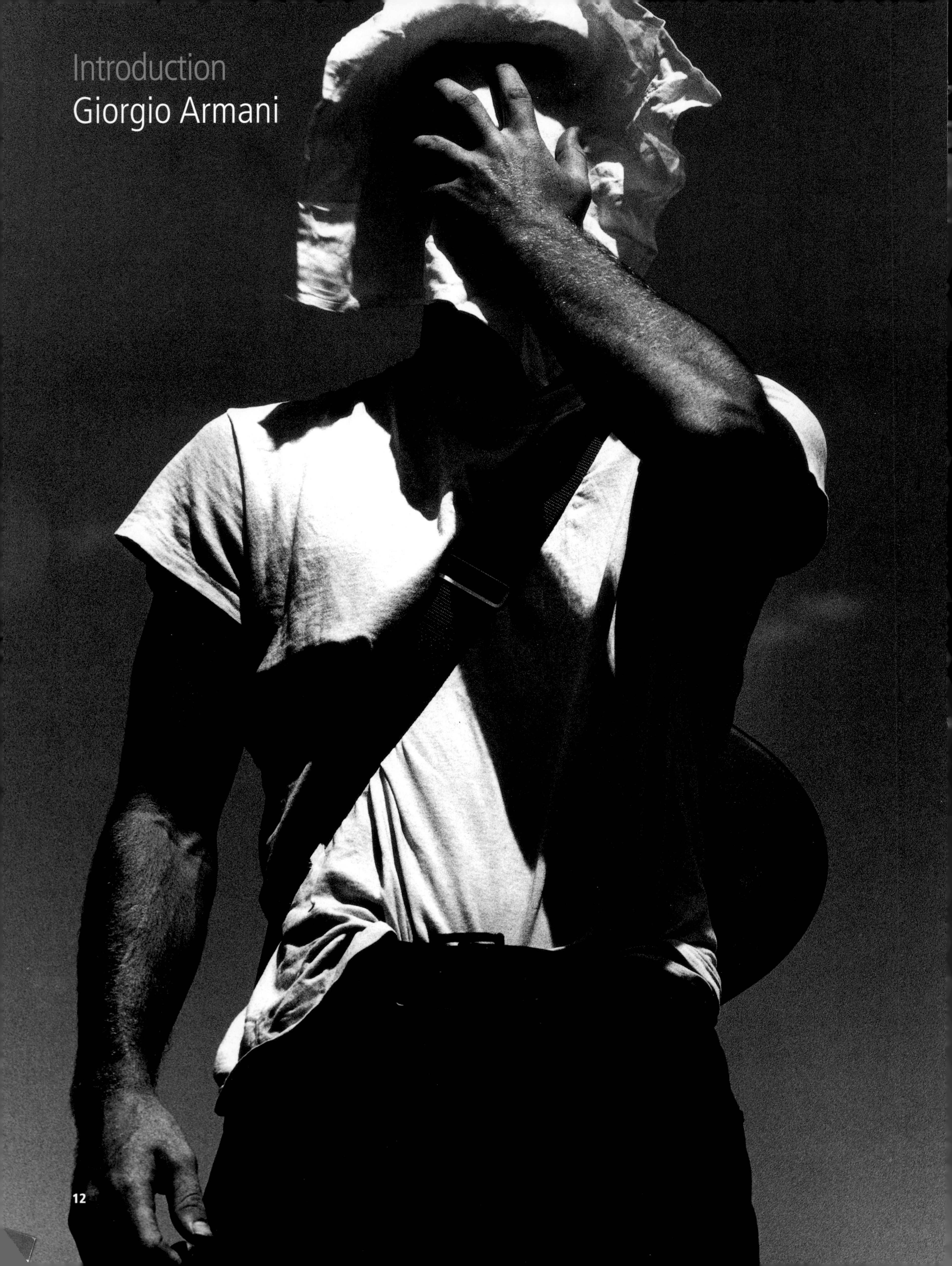

Introduction
Giorgio Armani

I've always thought of the T-shirt as the Alpha and Omega of the fashion alphabet. The creative universe **begins with its essentiality,** and, whatever path the imagination takes, ends with its purity.

What intrigues me about this piece of clothing – which has crossed our entire century unscathed and is poised for a glorious future – are the sensations that it transmits to me. The first is a **sense of cleanness** that goes beyond the superficial meaning of the word; it implies presenting oneself to others without artifice or disguise. The second, which may seem contradictory, is the **unabashed sex appeal** that this garment has like few others in the modern wardrobe: under a T-shirt, the beautiful bust of a woman or the handsome chest of a man are sculpted and desirable without becoming vulgar.

And then, I love the T-shirt as an **anti-status symbol,** putting rich and poor on the same level in a sheath of white cotton that cancels the distinctions of caste. It also excels as a **means of communication:** writings, drawings, poems, slogans, photos, worn as a way to tell the world who you are, what you think, where your ideals are directed.

Finally, I must confess it: despite the fact that some people think I am a man without vices, **I am a T-shirt addict.** It's the first thing that I put on in the morning and the last thing I take off at night!

Hero without a face, in an Armani T-shirt. Photograph by Albert Watson, 1988. **13**

A Sailor's Tale:

Origins of the T-Shirt

The measure of men: sailors' stripes on the high seas. 1942.

Slavery became even more common in the southern United States once the machine known as the cotton gin was invented by Eli Whitney, creating a huge surge in supply—and profits. By the 1850s King Cotton was America's leading export, worth more then all other crops combined, and the cheapest and most widely used textile fabric in the world. Photograph by L. Briscoe Allen, Port Gibson, Mississippi, circa 1906.

Top: Flowering cotton plant. *Gossypium*, which belongs to the mallow family, close cousin of the hibiscus, contains over thirty species of cotton — but only three have commercial use. *G. hirsutum*, or upland cotton, is the most common. Immediately after fertilization the cotton boll, which contains the seeds and seed fibers, forms. Six weeks later the boll bursts, and harvesting begins. From *Geology of Mississippi*, by B.L.C. Wailes, 1854.
Bottom: T-shirts go undercover at a Caribbean naval base. Circa 1944.

The story of the **most adaptable piece of clothing** in Western wardrobes stretches back to a time when the T, once underwear, was reborn as an overgarment. While its origins are murky, they begin with two creation myths: the tale of sailors and the sea, and the story of that most humble and noble fiber, cotton.

The history of men's underwear has its origins in the military. As far back as the eighteenth century, soldiers were issued, with their basic kit, no underpants, but a long-tailed shirt that wrapped between the legs in a diaper effect instead. Well-to-do civilians wore such undershirts, too, along with "britches liners," but these garments represented limited and defining **symbols of social caste** and fashion. This state of affairs lasted until the American Civil War, when soldiers were given a flat-woven wool shirt along with waist-to-ankle drawers.

About the same time, the U.S. Navy was issuing sailors a regulation set of bell-bottoms, topped off by jumper and undershirt. By 1880, that jumper achieved a V-neck opening, with the undershirt visible at the neck. Vestigial predecessor of the T-shirt, it was elbow and hip length and made of cotton flannel, and marked the **transition from woven to knitted T.** But unlike its modern equivalent, it had a placket with two buttons on the side of a collarette hemmed with binding. Sailors in the Spanish-American War were documented wearing such T-shirts, *sans* jumper, while working in the engine rooms or swabbing decks.

But these early appearances of the T were confined to the high seas. On shore leave the undershirt was less in evidence; winter uniforms were habitually worn with a wool dickey prior to 1908. It was highly irregular in the Victorian period in civilian clothes to have the neck exposed to the elements. The term **"leatherneck"** was coined around this time to describe sailors with characteristically open collars and unfashionably tanned skins.

On the civilian front, underwear moved on parallel lines. It still functioned principally as apparel worn underneath outer garments to help shield the body from the cold. For winter, woven silk, cotton, and wool of different weights were all manufactured. Rugged Australian lamb's wool (bulky and dyed olive brown) was perhaps the warmest on the world market, while summer underwear came in lightweight wool generally available in limited colors. (One manufacturer offered a choice between light ecru and camel's hair). In the less severe months, simple knitted cotton versions (known as balbriggans after the town in Ireland where they originated) were preferred.

In terms of style the undershirt had another antecedent. It owed **a nod to the tank** swimsuit that was so popular since the 1890s. The tank's enthusiastic reception marked a trend wherein underwear specialized for sports proliferated. By the turn of the century, the sight of **men in underwear in public places** became familiar, no longer fulminating.

The revolution in textiles had affected even the armed forces. In 1913 the U.S. Navy officially adopted a crew-necked short-sleeved version of the T to cover the chest hairs of its salty dogs. No longer flannel, it was knitted of cotton, without buttons, with a generous collar opening designed to be pulled over the head. This was a **crucial evolutionary change** for the T as we now know it. World War I was another instigator of change, as doughboys on the front clamored for a fabric other than wool, not for aesthetic reasons but for practical ones. Cotton or silk dried more quickly and offered a **promise of relative comfort** in the trenches.

While United States Marines, whose work requirements were akin to those of the Navy, moved quickly to embrace the T, it was the Navy's insistence on **seasonal clothing that set the pace,** the styles, and the trends for occupational clothing. By World War I, naval physical training for all recruits was conducted wearing Ts with the seamen's names stenciled on them.

The British Navy continued to set standards for navies around the world with its woven flannel T-shirt: wrist length in winter, above elbow length in summer. The story that the sailors were ordered to sew sleeves onto their shirts to spare Queen Victoria the **sight of hairy underarms at attention** has been disclaimed by historians at the Greenwich Maritime Museum, though the early acceptance of a T-shirt by the Royal Navy is well established.

Back on the civilian front, the 1920s initiated the union suit, also known as the combination suit, either in long- or short-sleeved styles. These long-bodied suits (which came to be known as "long johns" in colloquial parlance) were offered by manufacturers like Munsingwear and Sears, Roebuck & Co. The nainsook suit, a lightweight cloth of strong basketweave construction, joined them in popularity. But science was marching forward with changes that had repercussions for the T. By 1928 rayon had made its appearance, taking part of the underwear market from wool and cotton. The new fabric became especially popular in the **athletic styles favored by returning soldiers,** including sleeveless shirts with deep armholes. Soon the "singlet," offering ease of movement, comfort, and an attractive appearance, could be found in the wardrobe of most males. This helped to push the T further in the direction of general acceptance. By the 1930s Hanes, along with Sears, Roebuck, started producing undershirts with short sleeves and crew necks for about 24 cents apiece. With a nod to its nautical origins **they called their T a "gob shirt"** and, with a flash of foresight, announced its role as both inner and outer garment: "It's practical, correct either way."

But nothing galvanized the acceptance of the T like the last World War. The Japanese attack on Pearl Harbor had an immediate impact on the **12 million Americans who donned uniforms** almost overnight. By the following year the U.S. Navy sent out its official specs to suppliers for an all-cotton shirt with a round, moderately high neck, and short sleeves at right angles to front and back panels. Plain milky white at time of issue, they were **known in the vernacular as "skivvy" shirts.** It was the beginning of a legend—the T shortly saw so much frontline battle action that it became the emblem of manliness.

Thus the war in the Pacific was particularly crucial to the acceptance of the T as outerwear. It was a relatively informal war, sartorially speaking, and under the palm trees, in the heat and humidity, the T alone, worn with trousers, made plain common sense. Ts washed easily, they rolled up compactly, they **doubled as towels, shoe shine rags, pillows,** or bandages. The T occasionally also served a bravura purpose, as when a group of Marines stranded on the Solomon Islands were rescued by spotter planes after they tied their white Ts together as a signal flag. (Only a few months later in the war the rescue would have failed, since a sage-green camouflage T was **adopted for defensive reasons.**) Envious of the relaxed uniform style of its colleagues (and after convincing reports that the T **protected soldiers against burns and bugs**), the Army nevertheless waited until 1948 to adopt the quarter-sleeve undershirt, as it was officially known. "Like women with constricted undergarments and white gloves, they will never go back!" said Walter Bradford, curator of the U.S. National Museum of the Army.

By the late 1940s servicemen poured back home from overseas—and the T came with them. It became **the postwar uniform** and, in warmer climes, started the transition from under to outerwear. The war had given egalitarianism a new meaning, and the T was **worn with pride by men from all walks of life.** When newly minted U.S. Senator John F. Kennedy, movie-idol handsome, a millionaire and a war hero to boot, was photographed relaxing in a T-shirt in his Georgetown townhouse, **the T had, socially speaking, arrived.** The T-shirt now became the clothing of choice at the backyard family picnic, donned while dining with Mom and eating apple pie.

Almost as ancient in human history as war, and figuring as large in the lore of the history of the T, is the story of cotton. Today the T has been interpreted in virtually every substance, natural or man-made. Still, more than three-quarters of T-shirts made in the United States (the biggest global manufacturer of the T) start with cotton. Marco Polo reported on the flourishing cotton industry in India, dating from 6000 B.C., while in the New World, Mexican cotton was known by 5000 B.C., and in Peru by 2500 B.C. Today than more **seventy countries grow this vegetable** fiber, with China leading the pack with one-quarter of the world's production (nearly five million metric tons) and the U.S. in second place with one-fifth the world total. India, Pakistan, and Egypt are also important producers, as are the former Soviet republics of Uzbekistan and Kazakhstan. All over the world, cotton grows **at a latitude from 47 degrees to 30 degrees,** preferring fertile, well-drained moist soil and hot temperatures.

Cotton goes by the scientific name of *Gossypium* and belongs to the mallow family, close cousin of the hibiscus, the hollyhock, and okra. The genus contains **over thirty species of cotton** but only three have commercial use: *G. barbadense, G. herbaceum,* and *G. hirsutum.* The last of these is the most common and is generally referred to as upland cotton.

In the wild, **cotton is a perennial** (Columbus reported cotton growing in the Bahamas in 1492), but in cultivation it is planted annually from March to May and harvested in fall. A day in the life of cotton begins in the morning when the plant opens. Immediately after fertilization the cotton boll, which contains the seeds and seed fibers, forms. Three weeks later the fibers are mature. A layer of cellulose a day is added to their tubular walls until, twenty days on, the boll bursts. The cotton harvester now picks the dried bolls, while the spindle harvester gathers the lint and seeds.

Then cotton goes to the cotton gin, the machine whose ancestor, Indian charka, worked fine on *G. barbadense* cotton but not at all for upland cotton. It took Eli Whitney to figure out in 1793 how to adapt it. The gin had the perverse effect of making cotton a huge cash crop—and slavery even more common. By the 1850s **King Cotton was America's leading export,** worth more then all other crops combined—the cheapest and most widely used textile fabric in the world. **Cotton led to war** when Northern abolitionists challenged the slavery system that the cotton economy depended on for its profits. Since that time, the mechanics of producing cotton have remained largely the same. **To this day, the gin dries and cleans** the cotton, the gin stand cleans the lint, and the gin press molds the cleaned fibers into bales, which are then sent to spinning plants to make yarns, or exported.

A critical component to the history of cotton was the **development of tools and mechanics** for yarn and fabric production. Thirteenth-century Spain was the first place that cotton in the West was woven, spreading first to the Netherlands, then to England by the late sixteenth century. The next two hundred years witnessed the **birth of giant textile enterprises,** whose growth was spurred by technological milestones. Among these were John Kay's 1733 invention of the flying shuttle (the first step toward the modern loom), the first warp knitting machine in 1775, and Cartwright and Watt's first steam-powered textile mill in 1785. Cotton in Europe gained new commercial importance once America began to provide a steady **supply of raw material,** but it took Englishman Samuel Slater, who rebuilt a spinning frame from memory in Providence, Rhode Island, in 1790, to bring powered textile manufacturing to America. American John Sharp soon invented the ring spinning frame that is the basis of all modern machines (1828) and Isaac M. Singer perfected the sewing machine in 1851. The invention of automated machines in 1889 set in motion the duet between the T-shirt and cotton that continues today.

Now the story circles back to its beginning, back to the sailor and the sea. Until about 1825 ready-made clothing was available only in port cities, sewn in the "slop" shops of Boston and New Bedford for a boom market of sailors and whalers. The sailor's "gob shirt," a white undershirt worn for work, or beneath a jumper at formal occasions, was a popular garment. It was an idea whose time was about to come. Soon the **concept of ready-made, easy-fit** work clothes expanded inland, creating fertile ground for the proto T to develop.

Study of Quartermaster Clothing and Equipment for the Tropics

QUARTERMASTER BOARD PROJECT T-356

VOLUME 2

Reports of Individual Clothing and Chemical Treatments

CONDUCTED AT CAMP INDIAN BAY, FLORIDA, 15 JUNE TO 1 SEPTEMBER 1944

THE QUARTERMASTER BOARD, CAMP LEE, VIRGINIA

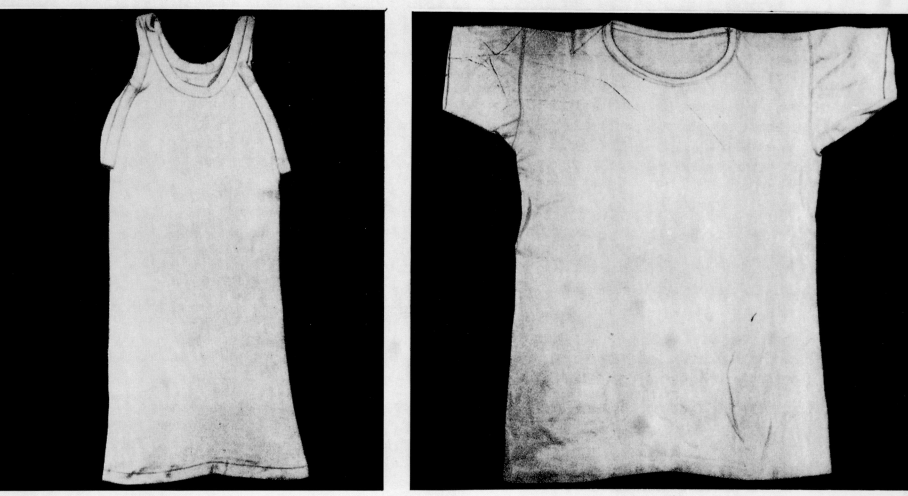

FIG. 73A

FIG. 73B

Description.

Item No. 217.—Knitted white cotton sleeveless undershirt of carded or combed cotton yarn, armholes and neck opening edged with ⅝" band of self fabric, ¾" hem at bottom either flat knit or 1 x 1 rib knit. (See Figure 73A.)

Item No. 218—Lightweight flat knit white cotton undershirt, high neckline, 5" sleeve with ¾" hem, ¾" band of self material stitched around neck opening, ⅞" hem at bottom. (See Figure 73B.)

Left and top: The U.S. Army recognized the T's effectiveness as a sun and bug screen years before its official adoption in 1948 as standard attire. 1942.

Bottom: Skivvies at attention: all aboard with the U.S. Navy. 1942.

23

The earliest authenticated T-shirt dates to 1913, when the U.S. Navy adopted a crew-necked, short-sleeved, white cotton undershirt to be worn under a jumper, designed to cover the chest hairs of sailors.

Calisthenics-by-the-sea: U.S. Army infantry shapes up in Atlantic City. Photograph by Fred He   circa 1942.

After being adopted by the rest of the armed forces the proto-T, baptized by the gas attacks and trench warfare of World War I, quickly became ubiquitous in civilian wardrobes.

LIFE

JULY 13, 1942 **10** CENTS
YEARLY SUBSCRIPTION **$4.50**

REG. U. S. PAT. OFF.

Above: The T-shirt gains cover status when worn by a U.S. Air Corps gunner. Photograph by Eliot Elisofon, Las Vegas, Nevada, 1942.
Right: Dice, poker, and downtime aboard ship. Circa 1944.

Left, top: Underwar: draftees don their basics. San Diego, California, 1942.
Left, bottom: The T takes center stage as U.S. Marines celebrate July 4th in the Philippines. 1943.
Below: In wartime, *everybody* rolled up their sleeves, even rock idol Elvis Presley. Fort Chaffee, Arkansas, 1958.

Above: The men who dropped the bomb: the crew of the Enola Gay shortly before the flight to Hiroshima. Marinas Islands, August 6, 1945.
Right: Bikini Atoll, 1946.

The Proletarian Uniform: Working Class Heroes

Blood, sweat, and near-tears. A worker rests after a day in the burning oil fields of Kuwait. Photograph by Sebastiao Salgado, 1991.

33

Men and monuments: steelworkers building Rockefeller Center, New York, 1932.

Above: Man and machine: the steamfitter as hero. Photograph by Lewis Hine, 1921.
Right: Dragging for bodies in the murky waters of New York. Photograph by Weegee, 1938.

Above: Genderless in trailer park America. Photograph by Steven Klein, Florida, 1995.
Right: "Salt and Pepper Angels," in the guise of New York City policemen. Photograph by Jill Freedman, 1979.

The ubiquitous T. Qutab Minar, New Delhi, India. Photograph by Mitch Epstein, 1981.

The T-shirt has always been a statement of social caste. As such, it takes its position solidly and defiantly on the side of the worker. The image is, in its historical essence, a deeply masculine one, whose emotional components turn on **independence and rugged individualism.** "A working-class hero is something to be," pronounced John Lennon in his song from the 60s. Both fiercely conservative and utterly socialist, patriotic, and subversive at once, the T-shirt seen on the back of a worker-hero is perceived as egalitarian in outlook; it rejects hierarchy and privilege and embraces the community of other men, other workers. English novelist Thomas Carlyle, in his famous diatribe on fashion, *Sartor Resartus*, anticipates the T-shirt's **resolutely antifashion** stance when he denounced "clothes-loving men who do not work."

And what does our hero wear? From the steel tips of his partially laced-up boots, his creased and molded blue jeans are adorned with a red bandanna, tucked into a rear pocket, topped off by his white T-shirt—rumpled, stained, torn, with one sleeve rolled for a pack of cigarettes. Dressed for a day of work at the factory or on the farm, he's **Adam after the Fall,** forthright and manly, vulnerable yet strong, unsophisticated but equal to anything.

Part of the facade of the American dream with its casual comfort, its functionalism, and its simplicity, the T-shirt's democratic connotations as antifashion catapulted it quickly to the proportions of a classic. Its practical material and adaptable shape fulfilled the requirements for working gear. It was **washable, durable, and cheap.** It was light enough to fit under outerwear, and it was absorbent enough to accommodate the beads of sweat or drenching rain that outdoor work required—yet still dry out in record time. The design grew even more practical when the shirtfront acquired a pocket to accommodate the worker's gear—whether pencils or chewing tobacco. The loose fit suited **ectomorphs as well as mesomorphs,** providing easy sizing, efficient mail-order, and forgiving shapes on work-hardened bodies.

In this guise as factory hero the T-shirt had its poster boys. On December 31, 1947, Tennessee Williams's play *A Streetcar Named Desire* had its premiere in New York City – and the T took top billing. Brando's sullen Stanley Kowalski flaunted his T with braggadocio, playing the factory worker arriving home and breaking out beers at the poker table. In the film version of *Streetcar* in 1951 the T was also the star, ripped and clinging to Brando's muscled torso after the critical rape scene like the humidity of a Southern night.

Brando's hunky physique was itself a testament to an enduring stereotype: the physical ideal of the **proletarian as strong man.** Muscle men have been popular in every culture, but particularly in the United States, where the culture of competition and militarism joined an admiration for athleticism. These predilections have been in evidence since the eighteenth century, visible in culture heroes ranging from President Andrew Jackson to Sylvester Stallone. The brawny build stood for America itself: **primitive, naive, and symbolic** of the brute triumph of man over nature. This *beau ideal* included familiar physical traits that even today grace Calvin Klein ads: broad shoulders, enlarged pectorals supported by defined intercostal muscles, and a perky gluteus. This fit body wasn't there just for posing; its incarnation was known for readiness to engage in out-and-out brawls, either for a good cause or in the blithe spirit of an honest punch-up. For all those muscles had a moral rationale as well: self-discipline and self-improvement (in the form of training or working out) was implied, as well as a role as agent of justice wherever brute force was required. Cinema strongmen like Arnold Schwartzenegger, Clint Eastwood, or Charles Bronson right wrongs and exact vengeance with fearsome efficiency, redeemed by their personal homespun humility.

That homespun quality has its **roots in the soil.** The T was once the sartorial province of the farm worker, to be worn under overalls of blue denim or heavy cotton. At the start of the century the T was one essential offering in the "wish books" of catalogue companies like Sears, Roebuck & Co., who advertised it as underwear. The saturation of these mail-order houses into rural communities had a great deal to do with the **wholesale adoption of the T** as a work shirt. The Farm Security Administration documented its ubiquity with a **legacy of rural Depression era** images that are imprinted forever on the collective consciousness. In them, gaunt-faced, weather-beaten men and women work the arid land uncomplainingly. Like modern-day Jobs, they suffer tornadoes and drought, locust plagues and bank repossessions in stoic silence. Their workaday clothes don't have the same molded, sweaty, armored look of the factory/union man – instead they are faded, dusty, patched, and wind-whipped, like some tattered flag of defiance.

The rural associations of the T and its universalizing message of the **dignity of work** were reinforced when it was adopted in marches and protests as the uniform of choice. This political meaning gathered steam with the civil rights and antiwar movements in America, the student revolts in 1968 in Paris, the antinuclear demonstrations in the U.K. in the 80s, and AIDS protests in the 90s. All adopted the clothing of the worker, identifying their **protests with the masses**. By doing so they joined a group that shares an identity – a tribe of protagonists in adversity, whose heraldic symbol became the T.

The factories have closed and the farms are fewer – but the T lives on. While traditional categories of work have narrowed in the twentieth century, the plain and simple, function-determining dress form of the worker continues to exert its appeal for all classes and occupations. T-shirts and jeans, **like peanut butter and jelly,** are a pairing that is as perfect in its simplicity as it is evident, filled with the nostalgia for being of and like the people.

By the 50s the T presided over a period of explosive growth and economic expansion in the West. As a **cultural record,** the T is one picture window (that 50s watchword in tract architecture) into what Marshall McLuhan called "expensive and influential programs of commercial education" that transformed the West into a material world. After World War II

Muscleman Jack Johnson in Mexico. Circa 1920.

the working class metamorphosed into a new booming middle class. Mass production took on a new urgency as the maws of capitalism needed to expand. Instead of the classic high-to-low approach to fashion, from couture to knockoffs, a **revolution was in the making.** Now the inspiration started to come, not from the Avenue Montaigne, but from the sidewalks of suburbia. Manufacturing maximized markets by targeting all socioeconomic levels at once, and soon designs increasingly **favored loose-fitting clothes** sized to accommodate the "average" figure. The garment industry worldwide defined progress by the development of synthetic fibers. Promising no more ironing and easy laundering (those last obstacles to democracy in dress), the new polyesters and rayons came precreased and wrinkle free. Cotton, formerly the province of the laborer, now moved on up as an upper-class prestige fabric.

Painted right into the bright postwar picture of split-level rec rooms filled with pod-shaped furniture and neon prosperity was the ubiquitous T. It continued to be **worn by the hordes of servicemen** returning from war, especially those who served in the Pacific, and also by their offspring, in record numbers. The huge baby boom between 1946 and 1957 — nearly 35 million births in the United States alone — created a new dynamic. The care and feeding of the very young dominated the landscape. Parenthood at these levels demanded time, requiring goods that saved energy. Enter the **wash-and-wear, slip-it-on, sleep-in-it,** all-purpose T.

By the time the tots became teens, car culture found the T at the wheel, when a vast program of government money to build highways accelerated the development of suburban communities. Rivers of concrete (perhaps the most influential socioarchitectural form of the century) took people from the dense neighborhoods of the cities to the postage-stamp green acres on their perimeters. And roadworks were **built by men in T-shirts** and used by people wearing them, driving shark-finned convertibles.

But if for most of the 50s the T-shirt's wholesale adoption was confined to children, there were two notable group exceptions. The Beats, like the Bikers,

favored T-shirts (along with leather in quantity) to twang a chord in alienated youth everywhere. They thumbed their nose at postwar materialism, at convention, at the science-driven optimism around them. They heard another siren: the grievances that David Riesman's book *The Lonely Crowd* chronicled. Even the 1961 Beatles (**working-class blokes** from Liverpool's mean streets before they went Mod and became scrubbed versions of themselves) riffed those existential questions when they sported black Ts and played the Mersey Sound Cavern Club.

By the 60s private convulsions about self and sexuality and the public trauma of wars and youth against old politics blew the lid off. That same identification with **outsider status** took the T-shirt on the road to Woodstock and the Haight, to Carnaby Street and the Boul' Mich, where it dressed a vision of communal love and freedom, spiritual eroticism, and intellectual and pharmaceutical inquiry. Embroidered, tie-dyed, decorated with beads, feathers, and flowers, the T was no longer a garment notable only for its worker plainness. And yet that tradition was its lodestar. As Ian Chambers said in *Popular Culture*, "**pop culture** may no longer be strictly working class as the idealistic purists of political formalism would like, but it does emerge from the inventive edges of consensus . . . [and] gestures through a widening democratization of styles."

That **T as Everyman** soon managed to infiltrate preppy Americana. Worn by up-and-coming Senator John F. Kennedy in Washington, D.C., in the 50s and two decades later by "working woman" Jacqueline Onassis on the streets of New York, its proletarian image had been subsumed by the upper classes as a recreational and leisure-time look. Now Ralph Lauren's "cowboys" in Ts and jeans lounge alongside old Ford pickup trucks; investment bankers don Ts and khakis when yachting; and German designer Jil Sander makes the world's most expensive T in gossamer silk. Carlyle may have had the last word on the wearing of the working-class T at the end of the millennium by the fashion-loving classes: "Clothes have made men of us; they are threatening to make clothescreens of us."

Night and day: the T in Spanish Harlem. Photograph by Joseph Rodriguez, 1987.

Above: The T's roots are in the soil: a white tenant farmer works shares in South Carolina. Photograph by Dorothea Lange, 1936.

48   **Above:** Men together, Italian style. *The Family,* Luzzara, Italy. Photograph by Paul Strand, 1953.
    Right: Men together, the American way. Gay Pride Day, West Village, New York. Photograph by Chantal Regnault, 1983.

Above: The starkness of the T and the embellishment of the tattoo. Photograph by Leon Levinstein, New York, 1958.
Right: Strange days: two boys and a dog, Coney Island. Photograph by Arthur Tress, 1969.

The extended backyard. Photograph by Bruce Davidson, Yosemite, California, 1966.

Portents and visions: suburban anomie in the West. Photograph by Garry Winogrand, New Mexico, 1957.

Dean, an
Springstee
The T-Shi
n Music a
Cinema

58 **Left to right, top to bottom:** Gary Cooper, Marilyn Monroe and Arthur Miller, Brigitte Bardot in *Babette Goes to War,* Charlie Chaplin in *Modern Times,* and Tony Curtis.

Left to right, top to bottom: James Dean; Art Carney, Jackie Gleason, and Audrey Meadows; Henry Winkler, aka "The Fonz," Clark Gable and Claudette Colbert in *It Happened One Night*; Rock Hudson; and the cast of *West Side Story*.

Above: Belting out the dashed dreams of the working class, Bruce Springsteen sounds a heartfelt chord in America. Photograph by Annie Leibovitz, New York, 1984. **Right:** The genius of soul in America, the Reverend Al Green. Photograph by Albert Watson, New York, 1992.

IN th
ed the heaven
and t
And th
orm, and void
and darkn
e of the deep
And the S
on the face o
the waters.
And God
ght: and there
was light.
And God
at it was good
and God divid
n the darkness
And God
Day, and th
e evening an
And God said
a firma
midst of the
it divide
aters from the waters
And God made the firmament, and divided
e waters which were under the firmament
om the waters which were above the firma-
ent: and it was so.

T is for Talkies

T-shirt roots are tangible in the history of film, and also run deep in the rambunctious and meandering world of music. Both music and cinema offer us ideals, models — **enhanced projections of who we are,** how we live, and what we look like — that resonate in larger-than-life ways with their audience. The reasons for this are multiple.

As cinema became increasingly concerned with *vérité*, it came also to reflect the man (or woman) on the street's habitual dress — or undress, in the T's case. The T marked the evolution of a certain androgynous, **artless appearance,** and, through the visual power of cinema, actually advanced that aesthetic. But the burgeoning presence of **the movie T started slowly** at first. The influence of the 1939 romantic comedy *It Happened One Night,* in which Clark Cable takes his shirt off, revealing not an undershirt but a bare chest, created economic havoc in the world of underwear, sending sales plummeting. World War II brought about a resurgence, and a host of war films like *Anchors Aweigh* (1945), the lively musical starring Gene Kelly (where the T danced animatedly on the high seas), helped the T reach a landlubbing public. Nurse Nellie Forbush and sailor chorus in *South Pacific* (1949) first brought Ts to Broadway. **War heroes were filmed in Ts,** arms akimbo, and the common man at home adopted the same cockily casual stance. The 1940 *Grapes of Wrath* featured the T, worn by desperate farmers on their exodus through the parched American West, as the **homespun, plebeian work clothing** it originally was.

In the 50s, film idol James Dean — with his dangling cigarette, white T-shirt, and motorcycle jacket in *Rebel Without a Cause* (1951) — set the National Angry Young Man standard, popularizing the **bad boy look.** Also responsible for the rise of the T were a trio of smoldering young actors — Montgomery Clift, Marlon Brando, and Paul Newman — all products of the Actors Studio, where they learned that a character's soul emerges through the expression of the body. What better surface to intensely translate emotion than the illusory T? When **Brando's T was ripped off** his

back in *A Streetcar Named Desire,* audiences swooned; when Newman, stripped to his T, advanced toward Patricia Neal in *Hud,* the sexual violence was transparent. Davy Crockett became the first TV-to-T star, while Art Carney added a twist of comic formality to a uniform of T and porkpie hat on the 50s TV show *The Honeymooners* (also starring Jackie Gleason), adding a vest to his character's down-home look. Even **Bogie donned a tropical armor T,** drenched in sweat and mud, to captain Katharine Hepburn downriver in *The African Queen* (1951).

As the 60s turned, Jean-Luc Godard's *À Bout du Souffle* (*Breathless*) starred chic, short-haired Jean Seberg strolling the boulevards in her *International Herald Tribune* shirt with louche-on-the-lam Jean-Paul Belmondo. Now the T became a **status symbol collectable** for the jet-set crowd. Andy Warhol's series of movies (*The Chelsea Girls, Lonesome Cowboys, Trash,* etc.) elevated the T to **camp classic.** The 1969 cult film *Easy Rider* with Peter Fonda and Dennis Hopper brought back the 50s look of T with motorcycle accessory — only the hair length had changed! Another repeated T-icon appears in film adaptations of Jean Genet's plays, especially Fassbinder's *Querelle* (1982), featuring a wider-necked shirt that owed a **nod to the French sailor's shirt.**

M.A.S.H., the 1970 saga of a fictitious frontline hospital during the Korean War, starred a military T emblazoned with logos — that only existed, Army historians confirm, in celluloid time. The **T took top honors** in 1979, winning Sally Field an Oscar for her role as union organizer in *Norma Rae.*

While it took Don Johnson in the TV series *Miami Vice* (1984-89) to create a **seriously grown-up image** for the T, pairing it with Armani suits in loose, flowing linen, *Thelma and Louise* (1991) undercut the **new formality** of the T-in-a-supporting-role with their picaresque, two-for-the-road gal outlaw film, where the T again turns its back on the status quo.

T's Top the Charts

If the T is a staple of cinema lore in the last half-century, nowhere is it more of a fixture than in the smoky cafes and stadiums of music culture. Son of the Blues and the Beats, the **T valorized the spontaneity of their music,** and became the backbeat of their stepchild, rock & roll. A veritable cotton chronicle of the music industry, as collectors of concert Ts can testify, the T has been a **showstopper at every major music happening,** from Monterey to Lollapallooza.

From Joe Cocker's tie-dyed T of Woodstock fame in 1969 to The Who's 1989 tour, to walking billboards for the career highlights of Led Zeppelin, the Grateful Dead, The Eagles, Pink Floyd, and Deep Purple, the range of the T-shirt is infinite. Still, its incarnations tend to divide into a few distinct categories. Most ubiquitous, the classic "portrait of the artist" is available for every singer or band, on sale at the arena nearest to you—all modeled on the top-of-the-T-shirt-chart, **all-time bestseller of Jimi Hendrix.** Equally totemic (if unimaginative) is the current album cover that sparked the tour, so that fans become walking promotion fences for the artists, with tour dates and cities inscribed on their backs. Another favorite style of heavy metal involves the skulls and dragons and gothic lettering that lurk on the shirts of bands like KISS, Metallica, AC/DC, Megadeth, and Black Sabbath. Kurt Cobain **T-shirts even function as tombstones,** with *The New York Times* obit and dates of the grunge saint's birth and death reproduced for eternally mourning fans.

One clarification is essential, however: when it comes to rockers, forget the white T. Three-quarters of rock Ts sold in the last twenty years came in only one color—deep, dark black. The San Francisco of the **psychedelic 60s gave birth to rock Ts** as we know them, a cottage industry at inception, but now a $500 million international market handily dominated by a half-dozen giant merchandising companies, many owned by major record labels. In the big picture, the U.S. consumes most music Ts, with the U.K., Japan, and Australia as runners-up. The $25 concert shirt typically is bought by 14- to 18-year-olds, and profits are split between the venue, the artists, and the manufacturer.

Seditionary in **slashed, ripped, and pierced Ts,** held together with safety pins and chains, punk ruled the 70s with angry outsider aura. Its raw, nihilistic performances revolutionized the idea of what rock & roll could be. Its music ancestors included druggie groups like The Velvet Underground and the trashy glam-rock New York Dolls, but **punk proper had a purer image.** Its ultimate incarnation was the band called The Sex Pistols, whose manager Malcolm McLaren, with designer Vivienne Westwood, ran a boutique called Sex that catered to alternative fashions. It was Westwood that first put the ragged punk T (borrowed from Richard Hell of Television) on the runways, a sequel to her shocking (in the U.K., anyway) T-shirt defacing "God Save the Queen" in Jubilee year. In its birthplace, England, punk was considered **dangerous to the fabric of society** and banned; by the time the underground spread to America it had spawned countless groups defined by the **sheer sonic force** of their music, like The Ramones, Patti Smith Group and, in a neo-pop offshoot, Blondie and Talking Heads. Harder, faster, LOUDER than other rockers, punk **addressed politics, sex, depression,** and society with a brutal realism—and with the T in shreds as their movement exploded.

Back in the 70s alternative bands wore T-shirts distinguished by bands around collar and sleeves. In the late 90s indie rockers like Kim Gordon of Sonic Youth brought that style back, and it sold briskly to the club crowd from the downtown Manhattan store, X Girl. And let's not forget the **white-trash baseball T** with three-quarter sleeves worn by bands like Boston, Rush, Dire Straits, and that rock legend (who moves between bands) Todd Rundgren. The music T now references its own short, if effervescent, past.

Why the rage for T-shirts? More than memorabilia or professions of fanhood, they are veritable **passports to self-invention.** From surf music to garage rock, from psychedelia to punk, the T associates the wrapper [sic] with its contents.

Left: Kim Basinger, fully dressed in pearls and an XL. Photograph by Herb Ritts, 1989.
Above: Antonio Banderas cools down his steaming torso. Photograph by Philip Dixon, 1990.

Above: Steve McQueen speaks his mind on China's Yangtze River in *The Sand Pebbles*, 1966.
Opposite, left to right, top to bottom: Mickey Rooney and son; Mr. and Mrs. Humphrey Bogart plus pooch; Jean-Paul Belmondo and Jean Seberg in *Breathless*, 1959; Gene Kelly in *Thousands Cheer*, 1943.

67

Above: The mellow, smoky sounds of trumpeter Chet Baker. Photograph by Herman Leonard, New York, 1956.
Right: Dawn after an all-night party in Sammy Davis, Jr.'s room at the Hotel Pennsylvania. Photograph by Burt Glinn, New York, 1959.

Left: Soul diva Diana Ross exudes star sensuality. Photograph by Albert Watson, 1992.
Above: Michael Jackson, pop's changeling prince. Photograph by Herb Ritts, 1992.

Above: Terence Trent D'Arby sounds a note of gritty, urban funk. Photograph by Matthew Rolston, Los Angeles, 1988.
Right: Sinead O'Connor as Celtic priestess, crying in the wilderness. Photograph by Matthew Rolston, Los Angeles, 1990.

Above: Debbie Harry and Chris Stein rocking to the sounds of their new wave band Blondie. Photograph by Lynn Goldsmith, New York, 1978.
Right, clockwise: Balladeer Tom Waits; reggae crooner Bunny Wailer; and legendary Grateful Dead guitarist Jerry Garcia.

Above: John Travolta wearing the uniform of the urban cowboy: T, jeans, and ten-gallon hat. Photograph by Annie Leibovitz, Los Angeles, 1980.
Right: Richard Gere plays an amoral punk on the lam in the 1983 remake of the classic French New Wave film, *Breathless*.

Above: Pretty woman Julia Roberts. Photograph by Herb Ritts, 1992.
Right: Macho and muscles in a classic 50s combination: T-shirt, leather jacket, and jeans worn à la Arnold Schwarzenegger. Photograph by Greg Gorman, 1989.

Sex and Sports: The T-Shirt Gets Physical

Strip-T-ease. Photograph by Arthur Tress, New York, 1979.

Above: Love in the streets. Photograph by Guzman, New York, 1993.
Right: Violent, predatory sex underlines the encounter between Paul Newman and Patricia Neal in the 1963 film, *Hud.*

By nature and design the T-shirt taps a common vein of sexuality. Whether crude, raw, and primal or free, floating, and ephemeral, it incorporates **animal sexuality** and **erotic appeal** with the heady intoxication of imagination.

The T's basic instincts lie first in its appearance as an "intimate body fashion"(as the apparel business refers to underclothes). Present in all clothes to a degree, the innuendo increases the closer the bodily connection: the nearer the skin, the headier the sexual scent. So the T's **torso-hugging dance** with the flesh feigns concealment while stimulating sexual curiosity. Tight, it emphasizes muscle beneath; loose, it suggests the flow of the naked form itself.

While the T's first transgression is to flaunt its transformation from underclothes, it also ruptures other rules of social decorum. Claudia Brush Kidwell of the National Museum of American History noted, "The emergence of the T shirt. . . **violates taboos** against cross-dressing and against male sexual display."

Sexual ambiguity has always been a potent theme in fashion, especially in modern clothing. Women wearing men's clothes is intrinsically an erotic act, just as men wearing women's clothes has coexisted apace. **Wholly masculine in origin,** the T was first adopted by women in the 60s as an Aquarian uniform for a horizon of peace and love. By the 70s, it was seized as a **gender-free flag** of liberation by another wave of women, and since has continued to acquire a whole vocabulary of forms, whether pure or provocative. Its essential neutrality stems from its look of streamlined function, and its implication of non-sexual uncorruptedness. But androgyny plays two ways: it suggests both a *1984/Brave New World*-style **unisex regimentation** and the older idea that sexuality may be richer if erotic affinities rather than differences are emphasized and shared. Whatever the leaning, the T is the clothing of choice.

The T undoubtedly caters to male sartorial fancies, stripped bare. It hearkens to the **ideal of the muscular,** developed body, a Western cultural icon born in ancient Greece. Greek gods and goddesses evolved in the shape of certain archetypes: Hercules became the broad-shouldered symbol of achievement—the Superman—through amazing exploits. Other gods assumed more intellectualized forms: Athena, goddess of wisdom, was tall, slender, and clad in **clinging, diaphanous drapery,** while Apollo was often interpreted in the developing body of a graceful pubescent boy. The T may also have antecedents in the Roman cuirass, a muscular breastplate made of leather that transformed the most unpretentious of upper bodies into the embodiment of authority. (That said, the T has limited value when the chest underneath is deficient in muscles and curves.) In any case, the T shows an ancient appreciation for **fitness, health, and the young,** and its approximation to the body links the wearer to a godlike self-ideal.

With a nod to its ancient forebears, the body modeled on Greek sculpture also became an **object of homosexual attention,** and that in turn helped codify this familiar shape: deep chest, shapely pectoral muscles, strongly defined hips, slim waist, jutting buttocks, and powerful thighs and calves—the characteristics that came to define the Western demigod.

Costume historians such as James Laver have argued that fashion focuses on different parts of the body to **prevent sexual boredom.** Laver claims that's why, in the 30s, backs were the focus of dresses; and why, over the last century, hemlines have shot up and down. The T, too, has shrunk and expanded with the vagaries of style, and each permutation has its focus. The cropped T focuses on the midriff and, at its most daring, the belly button. A **naked provocation,** its referents include the bikini and the harem costume of the exotic belly dancer. Furthermore, it opens a ground of **erotic risk** for adornments like piercing rings, tattoos, and other toys of fantasy.

The comic strip ideal of broad-shouldered, wasp-waisted men in clinging Ts was matched by buxom beauties like this Vargas girl. Illustration by Alberto Vargas, circa 1946.

Pinup dreams of a Parisian type, known affectionately to intimates as Jacques, Tongue de Velours (Jack Velvet Tongue).
Photograph by Robert Doisneau, 1936.

The oversized T connotes a different sort of **bodily freedom.** Born in urban streets and favored heavily by the preteen crowd, it doesn't differentiate between sexes and denies socioeconomic gaps. Its parody of fit, hanging knee-length on some wearers, eliminates any suggestion of adult sexuality, and offers a chadorlike refuge for adolescent modesties and prurience. Best of all, the XL-T simultaneously functions as an antiparental *and* **antitailoring protest.**

Flesh and the word come together in the Bible, so it is no surprise that sex and text go together on the T like cigarettes and scotch. It was the Navy that first emblazoned a lexical message across the formerly unicolor T, discovering, perhaps, that its straight lines went well with the swirling tattoo art on sailors' biceps. The association of the **macho military man** at boot camp with the skin-tight undershirt was an irresistible springboard for the logo T. Soon bravura **messages were flashing on chests** around the world, ranging from wistful to raunchy. From California: "So many girls… so little time." From a college fraternity in New Orleans: "9 inches." And from Amsterdam: "Beat me, whip me, tell me that you love me — then get the fuck out." Whether blatant or subliminal, they made the wearer feel the swashbuckling, **swaggering security** that armor might have conferred in another century. The heyday of the **sexy signboard** was indisputably the 70s, but even today, the message and the medium frequently meet.

Yet another permutation of the T's ability to articulate **sex on the body** lies in the black T, born in the 50s, which projected raw danger and adrenaline-pumping lawlessness onto the **honest workingman's garment.** Black meant young, black meant bad, black meant rebel. And, given the presumption of certain tastes, black was darkly, sultrily sexy. Even at its beginnings, Beat poets and abstract artists favored it above all hues. Black was the color of night, of the romantic, of dandies in velvet — ascetics and aesthetes alike. By the 60s it was political: the flag of Black Power. Soon it came to be identified with music, and rock & roll especially, where the **outsider value** of black had special credence. Black has never faded in its utter cool, and erogenous allure.

Whether waves, water balloons, hydrants, or fizzing champagne provide the moisture, the **second skin** of warm weather is the wet T. A collegiate perennial, it more than celebrates the body — it splashes praise up and down the beach. Emphatically not as natural as nakedness, its thinly disguised skin-structure **exalts the flesh.** Of course in these ultraviolet years the waterlogged T does have a protective function for rarely exposed zones, but no one sporting a wet T is deluded by that rationale. The shirt's sexuality has now superseded its androgyny and the wet T is a **progenitor of today's fashion** T, where design is about silhouette as much as attitude, about the way the shirt reveals breasts or biceps in a deceptively simple, streetwise way. It takes many forms, from ultraluxury to sheer minimalism. The relation of T to body has never been so tight.

As Anne Hollander said in *Sex and Suits*: "For modern clothes **sexuality became the fundamental expressive motor,** the underlying source of creative play." Offering up suggestive slices of before and after moments, Calvin Klein's ads of young men with shirts half off, or boxer shorts slipping off their hips, create the drama of a dreamlike, unfinished encounter. Guess Jeans launched Claudia Schiffer's star with an Ellen Von Unwerth photograph of the model emerging from water with a wet T-shirt clinging to her voluptuous physique. Even the Gap **sexed up** its high-collared classic pocket T with its context: Naomi Campbell standing coyly in short-shorts with hands between inner legs in a photograph by Steven Meisel. The T began as a second skin, and continues to function on the assumption that **objects of desire** have more suggestive power when clothed.

Above: The beau ideal. Illustration by Gianni Versace, Milan, 1996.
Right: Bulging pectorals and thrusting shoulders define the T as interpreted by cult artist Tom of Finland. 1965.

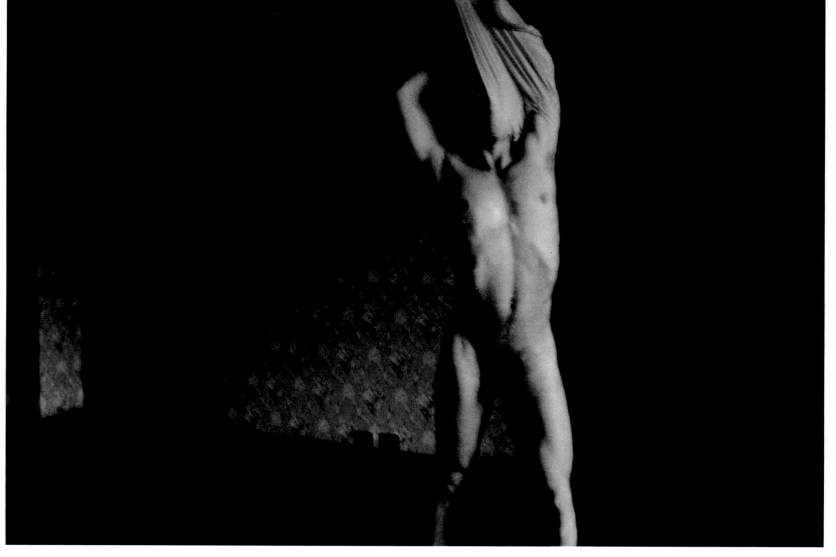

He was unaware that at the exact moment he removed his
undershirt, his body had grown to its perfection.
With his next ~~breathlessly~~ breathe, the moment had passed.

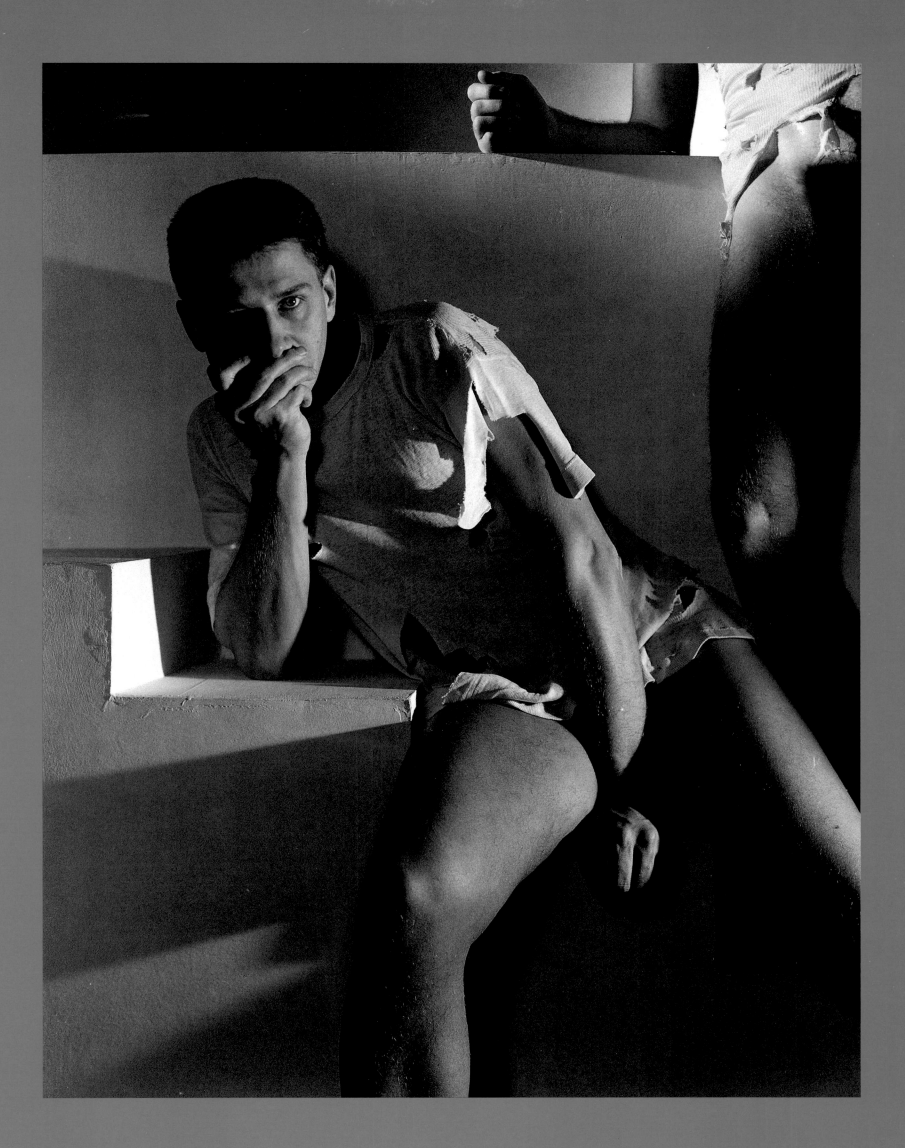

Left, top: *Two Boys on a Beach #1.* Etching by Paul Cadmus, 1938.
Left, bottom: Dream Sequence. Photograph by Duane Michals, 1978.
Above: Painters, lovers, and friends, Paul Cadmus and Jared French. Photograph by George Platt Lynes, New York, 1938.

Left: Last tango. Photograph by Andrea Blanch, Paris, 1991.
Above: Rise and Monty kissing. Photograph by Nan Goldin, New York, 1988.

Stagefront frenzy at the Rolling Stones' *Tattoo You* tour. Photograph by Michael Halsband, Orlando, Florida, 1981.

Clockwise: College rowing team, 1890; German gymnasts in San Francisco. Photograph by John Gutmann, 1935; Athletic hurdles, circa 1925.

Top to bottom: Swimmers. Photograph by Jacques-Henri Lartigue, Cap d'Antibes, France, 1932; Stickball gang. Photograph by William Klein, New York, 1955.

Left: Dancer Mark Morris, synthesizing fluid form. Photograph by Annie Leibovitz, New York, 1989.

Above: Blood and sand in the bullring. Photograph by Sabine Weiss, Avignon, France, 1960.

Above: Grace, speed, and strength: baseball legend Mickey Mantle. Photograph by Hy Peskin, Yankee Stadium clubhouse, New York, 1956.
Right: The three graces: tackle Dick Modzelewski with Giants teammates. Photograph by Robert Riger, Yankee Stadium, New York, 1958.

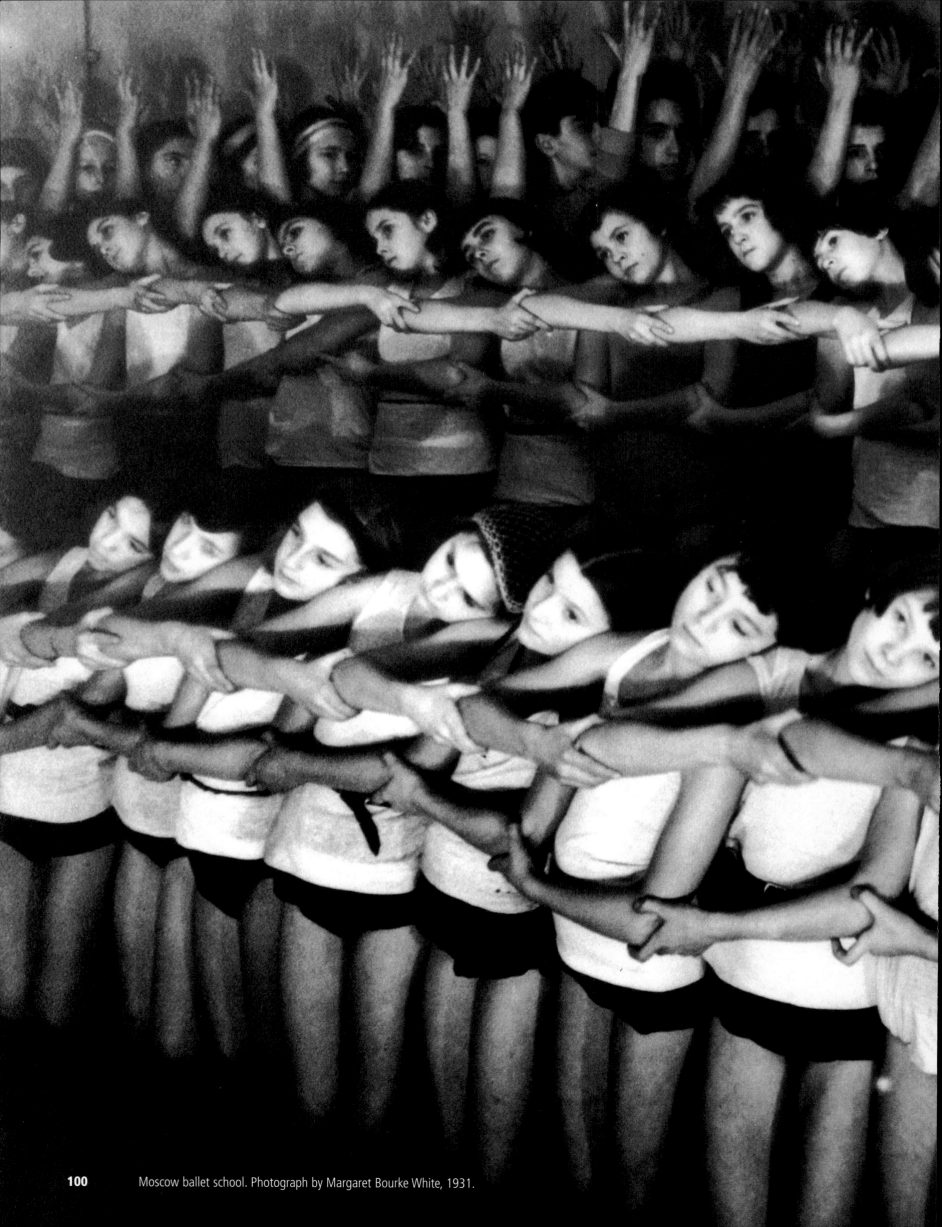

Moscow ballet school. Photograph by Margaret Bourke White, 1931.

Feathers flying. Photograph by Michael Thompson, 1995.

T-Shirt à la Mode: Fashion and Anti-Fashion

Left: Renée, chic in white T, August in Biarritz. Photograph by Jacques-Henri Lartigue, France, 1930.

Above: The Kenosha Klosed Krotch suit, early predecessor of the T-shirt. Jockey International advertisement. 1910.

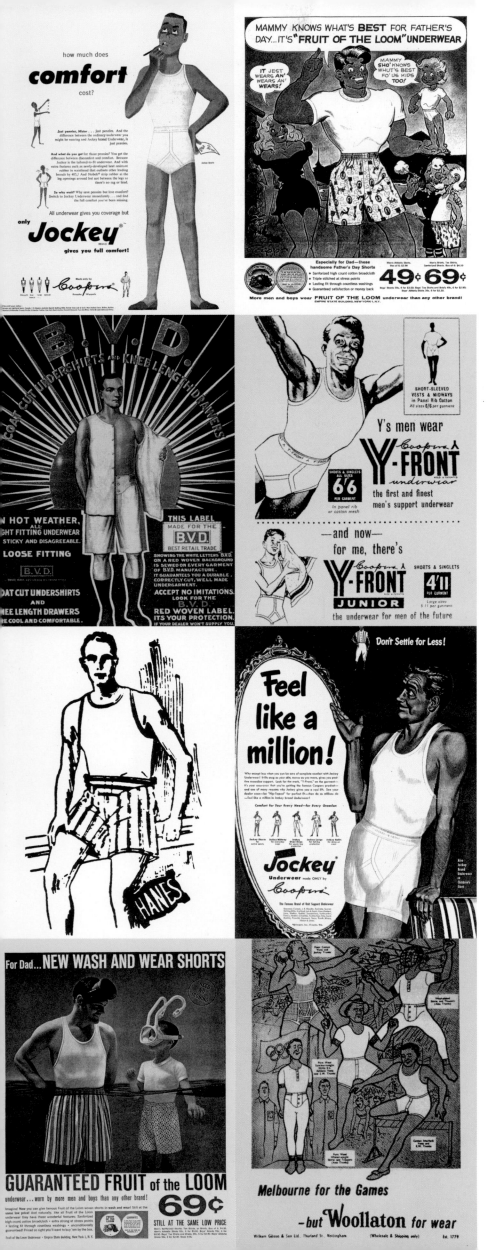

"The single most powerful fashion **metaphor of the century,**" pronounced *Vogue*; "The little white wardrobe wonder," lauded *Harper's Bazaar*; "Incontestably the shirt of today," agreed *Elle*. Modest and utilitarian at its start, this piece with a past has evolved to become the **determining garment** of a refashioned way of life.

Its earliest appearance in fashion came in the 1840s as a **woolen undervest** to protect women venturing to play sports. By 1880 Dr. Gustav Jaeger's publication "Sanitary Woolen System" launched undershirts as fashion. Sears, Roebuck in 1897 offered proto-Ts in Egyptian cotton and by the 1900s in silk with lace trimmings. But just as they began to get stylish in the 30s (using newly invented rayon to make vests **"skin-slim"**) the bra replaced **undershirts** as the foundation of choice.

Nevertheless, by 1951 the T was back. *Life* magazine noted the shirt "had gone high fashion...appearing on city streets and country club porches—and even at formal dances." **First sporty, then sensual,** now sensible, 15 million dozen were sold in that year (still a far cry from the 5 billion mark hit in 1995, putting T-consumption on a par with fast-food burgers). The T had become the leisure **counterpart of the little black dress** in postwar years. Ts were now mass-marketed not only in cotton but in manmade polyester, brought to life by Du Pont in 1953. Walt Disney and Roy Rogers saw the **possibilities of T-souvenirs** around this time, and with the 1959 invention of "plastisol," a more durable, stretchable ink, T-printing as we know it took off. Part of this explosion was due to the meeting of **advertising and the chest,** when sometime in the 60s, a picture of a Budweiser beer bottle graced the T-shirt for the first time. Corporation logos were not far behind—the **sponsored shirt** was born, aided by new technologies that made the mass production of full-color images on cloth possible. Capitalism soon smelled cash and volume manufacturers like the big three of Ts—Fruit of the Loom (including the BVD label), Hanes, and Jockey—began to produce preprinted shirts.

Left, top to bottom, left to right: Jockey ad in *Saturday Evening Post*, 1930; BVD ad in *Vanity Fair*, 1929; Hanes ad in *Vanity Fair*, 1929; Fruit of the Loom ads in *Saturday Evening Post*, 1957; Lyle and Scott ad, 1930; Jockey ad, 1950; Woollaton ad, *Draper's Record*, 1956.
Above: Just the basics. Kate Moss. Photograph by Corinne Day, 1993.

The sporting look of the T explains its evolution from softball uniform to Chanel; by the early 60s California designer Jax of Beverly Hills was adding gloss to sports Ts. **Color appeared on Ts for the first time,** before the protest lifestyle and sexual revolution of the late 60s added New Age spin to the T. With beads, peace patches, and embroidery à la Janis Joplin, and sporting text, it became **a worn signifier** of political beliefs and apocalyptic postmodern visions. Just as every dog has its day, every T had its slogan, and while students around the world marched in the streets, the T **doubled as a mask** when the tear gas canisters were fired. In the lackluster 70s an austere version was adopted by Gloria Steinem as an acceptable **uniform of feminism.** Yet the best-selling T to date was still cheesecake: a shot of 1976 poster girl Farrah Fawcett generated $8 million for its maker. In 1973 *WWD* declared the folkloric, **label-flaunting** T-shirts of the 70s, "the year's number one status symbol." Even doyenne of mode Jackie O. wore Ts in her working woman rebirth.

The mutation from **undergear to everywhere** channeled a radical revamping of the locker room staple, shrinking it to kid-size versions or stretching it into long dresses (early Betsey Johnson) or slashing it, *Flashdance*-style (1983). Norma Kamali created a hybrid bathing suit-with-attached-T. Agnes B. cut her T's closer to the body and made them **French fashion necessities.** "One generation's lingerie may become another generation's visible clothing," Richard Martin and Harold Koda point out in *Infra-Apparel* at the Metropolitan Museum in 1993. Calvin Klein's 80s ads by Bruce Weber proved it, redesigning the men's tank for the female form. Meanwhile, across the Atlantic, Karl Lagerfeld took the undershirt based on the French working man's *marcel*, appliqued it with Chanel C's, and made it the most knocked-off and illegally sold garment in the world.

British designer Katharine Hamnett turned T-fashion Pinto **agitprop** with a series of political shirts in the 80s (and wore a disarmament message T, "58%

don't want Pershing," to meet Maggie Thatcher). By the 90s, **fashion charity was exploding,** with "Nuclear-Free Pacific" Ts by Regan Cameron and breast cancer Ts, initiated by Ralph Lauren and the New York-based CFDA. A Hanes T-shirt auctioned on March 7, 1995 to benefit the Olympics netted $26,000.

The **oversized homeboy Ts** of the 90s existed alongside the shrunken Ts on grown-up torsos. Gianni Versace and others cut the T at **navel latitudes,** imitating the football jerseys of hot weather teams. Nearly every designer in the 90s has taken this **essential nothing** and made it a Something—in every material under the sun, including a substance called PET, made of recycled soda pop bottles. The Gap (in the 80s still a small San Francisco company) set out on a mission to make style affordable and taste inevitable for the masses, and took its **one-pocket T to double-digit profits.** Naomi Campbell summed up the T's ubiquity as "Americans' **summer uniform.**" Statistics say Yea: the average American owns eight Ts.

Born poor and anonymous, proclaiming the values of the lower class (not upper fringe), the T has nonetheless always flirted with fashion. Whether it acts as a **camera of who we are** and where we are going, a commemorative calendar of dress, a dialectic across the gender line, or even a simple assertion of the **skin-shirt nexus,** the T is the canary in a coal mine of taste. And, just as Coco Chanel predicted a half-century before, the moneyed classes now ape the lower ranks by adopting this 100 percent cotton stuff of the zeitgeist. Whether they purchase Comme des Garçons or Jil Sander versions selling for hundreds, or the more accessible offerings of Hanro or J. Crew, they have claimed the status of purity, abstraction, pristine form—**essential classicism.**

As the millennium approaches, has the T at last explored all its options? *Tabula rasa* for graphic messages that speak louder than words, the T has been slashed and ripped, beaded and gilded, ribbed and beribboned, shrunken and oversized, tie-dyed and eroticized. In the end the immutable whiteness of the once and future T—**utterly functional, simplicity itself**—remains, a bellwether of what lies ahead.

Right: Timeless, ageless style: twenty years ago Lauren Hutton dressed exactly the same, in a classic combination of T and jeans. Photograph by Steven Meisel, New York, 1993.

Left: Roughing it up: Linda Evangelista dons Chanel with black leather, chains, and a white T. Photograph by Peter Lindbergh, 1991. **111**
Above: Flamboyant and flowery, the T in a bed of roses. Illustration by J. Perez.

Left: Cindy and Shaq in an extra-small and an extra-large. Photograph by Matthew Rolston, 1994.
Above: Mute T: Kristen McMenamy and friend as mimes, New York. Photograph by Peter Lindbergh, 1993.

Left: The punk look and the T share a certain affinity. Photograph by Didier Malige, 1990.
Above: In summer, the landscape brightens and primary colors rule. Here, the T-shirt red and white, against fields of blue.
Photograph by Patrick Demarchelier, 1993.

Male model Tyson (in a computer-generated image) zooms off the page in *Vibe*. Photograph by Christian Witkin, 1995.

ACT UP (AIDS Coalition to Unleash Power) demonstration at the National Institutes of Health. Photograph by Brian Weil, Bethesda, Maryland, 1990.

The Canvas of History:

The T in Politics and Art

Above: Teenagers march from church to mourn the assassination of NAACP leader Medgar Evers. Jackson, Mississippi, 1963.
Right: The white supremacist movement in the United States started with small bands of adherents, but gained ground and force in the last decade.
Photograph by Rick Friedman, 1981.

Talking T

In an election year the T-shirt in the United States is as **visible as the American flag.** A pollster's dream source for studying ongoing trends, it champions candidates, even while disembowelling their faux pas and foibles. The 1992 election spawned a host of memorable Ts. A "Read My Lips, No New Taxes" T succinctly summed up George Bush's fidelity to his 1988 campaign promise: "Not." Dan Quayle's most repeated malapropism, "What a Waste it is to Lose One's Mind," was saved for posterity, while Bill Clinton came in for severe ribbing with "The Clinton Agenda: Sex, Drugs, and Rock n' Roll." There was even a call for the resurrection of a candidacy: "Tan, Rested, and Ready: Nixon for President 1992." When the **hats go in the ring, the T goes on the back.** It's election year once again!

The T became a comfortable bedfellow of politics in the late 40s (a child's T saying "Dew-It with Dewey" in the collection of the Smithsonian is a relic of the governor's failed campaign against Harry Truman), and has remained so ever since. In the mid 60s its **radical chic** was certified when SNCC (Student Nonviolent Coordinating Committee) chose a khaki T and jeans as their uniform in solidarity with the rural and working-class origins of blacks and other oppressed citizens. During the Vietnam era, the T was a **picket sign for an end to militarism** and a chant to peace, love, and understanding. Print and polemics had found their ideal medium in the T. The advent of self-silkscreened Ts in the 70s sent up a firestorm: soon, everyone was airing their **opinions on their chest.** Satirist Fran Leibowitz decried the new outspokenness in her 1978 book, *Metropolitan Life*: "If people don't want to listen to you, what makes you think they want to hear from your sweater?" (She was wrong — that year alone, about 500 million T shirts were sold in America.) The T was an urban ice-breaker, a party opener, a declaration of principles and individuality.

An exhibition held at New York's Fashion Institute of Technology, "T Line," curated by Richard Martin in 1992, charted one year in **T-shirt political history.**

Patriotism in 1991 was flying high with the Gulf War gearing up: "This Scud's for You" and "Iraq Cafe: a Great Place to get Bombed." The dangers of racism were alluded to in "David Duke For Governor," while a "Here Come Da Judge" T spoofed Supreme Court Justice Clarence Thomas's sexual harassment tightrope. The "Go Gorby" T-shirt seemed a signpost of the **ephemera of the T** — the Russian leader was soon erased from public life. The women's movement sported some unorthodox sentiments like "A woman needs a man like a fish needs a bicycle." Within 24 hours of the Rodney King beating, a T-shirt appeared with the L. A. police motto, "To Serve and Protect," over a body outline — just in time for the riots.

The New Statesman (October 4, 1991) reported a black market high in China for **dissident T-shirts.** With a subtle irony known as "pointing at the mulberry while swearing at the locust," the Ts convey the same meaning as the banners of Tiananmen Square. "I'm fed up — leave me alone" says one, "Can't blame society — it's the luck of the draw," said another sarcastically. In apartheid-torn South Africa, T-shirts bearing the slogans of 47 different antigovernment groups were, at one point, banned by police. Whether **the issue is racial discrimination, homelessness,** environmental protection, AIDS, or breast cancer, the T sends out the word unequivocally.

The T in Art

If the 50s were the **formative years of the T-shirt,** its most generous acceptance was found in the vibrating life-force of that decade's art world. In the literary corner were the Beats, those proto-hippies fomenting a holy, drug-hazed underground. And on the visual scene, Abstract Expressionism deified the idea of painting as an "act," a pure and unencumbered gesture, existential in time. Like the T itself, poetry and art extolled **the values of freedom of expression,** of spontaneity and of accident, the flux of things. The T and this art tempo had three qualities in common: emotionally charged physicality, the shock of the new,

Right, top: Cigars for T-shirts? Fidel Castro at the United Nations in New York. Photograph by Karen Ranucci, 1979.
Right, bottom: Lee Harvey Oswald being transferred from jail to the homicide bureau after the assassination of President John F. Kennedy. The photograph was taken moments before Oswald's own violent death at the hands of Jack Ruby. Dallas, 1963.

and the rigor of pure ideology. Jack Kerouac and William Burroughs, Allen Ginsberg and Ken Kesey were out on the road in California, on the Bowery, or in Tangier, **dressed in cool self-confidence and Ts.** And Willem de Kooning, Jackson Pollock, Frank Stella, and Ellsworth Kelly advertised their masculine bravura, their hard-drinking, rough-loving, high-risk lifestyle and bruising physical approach to their own painting while smearing paint across canvas, habitually in stained, ripped and torn Ts.

The 60s Pop movement was born out of this milieu and shared the same subversive nonconformity. The work of James Rosenquist, Larry Rivers, Jim Dine, Tom Wesselman, Roy Lichtenstein, Alex Katz, and David Hockney **elevated commercial culture to high art** by offering sustained attention to the material circumstances of life, with hyperrealizations of the ordinary, as in Claes Oldenburg's immense baggy sculptures. All kinds of subject matter were fused in a candid **confrontational realism.** Pop was popular, ironically so, but ambivalent about its sources in mass-mediated imagery. It unraveled the gender-marked 50s, substituting self-mocking comic book imagery and, in Andy Warhol's case, a committed interrogation of **masculine and feminine as masquerade.**

After a decade-long lull, an explosion of small neo-movements – whether Neo-Expressionism, Neo-Geo, Neo-Conceptualism, Neo-Minimalism or Neo-Pop – characterized 80s art, manifest in the Day-Glo splatterings of Jean-Michel Basquiat, Keith Haring, and Kenny Sharf, or the cooler, enigmatic work of Eric Fischl, Julian Schnabel, Cindy Sherman, and Ross Bleckner. In the **high-rolling boomtown atmosphere** of the heady 80s, art and fashion were the hottest coupling. Artists not only attended fashion shows or appeared in ads but staged their own catwalk shows, like Matthew Barney in his Rotterdam retrospective in 1995. The T worn by artists, used by them as a canvas, or depicted in their work embraced the end-of-the-millennium conundrum of the artist who cannot make art but only refer to it. In this world of unreal things, the T shirt, replaced by signs and images of reality, as high priest Jean Baudrillard intones, is **becoming something other than it is.**

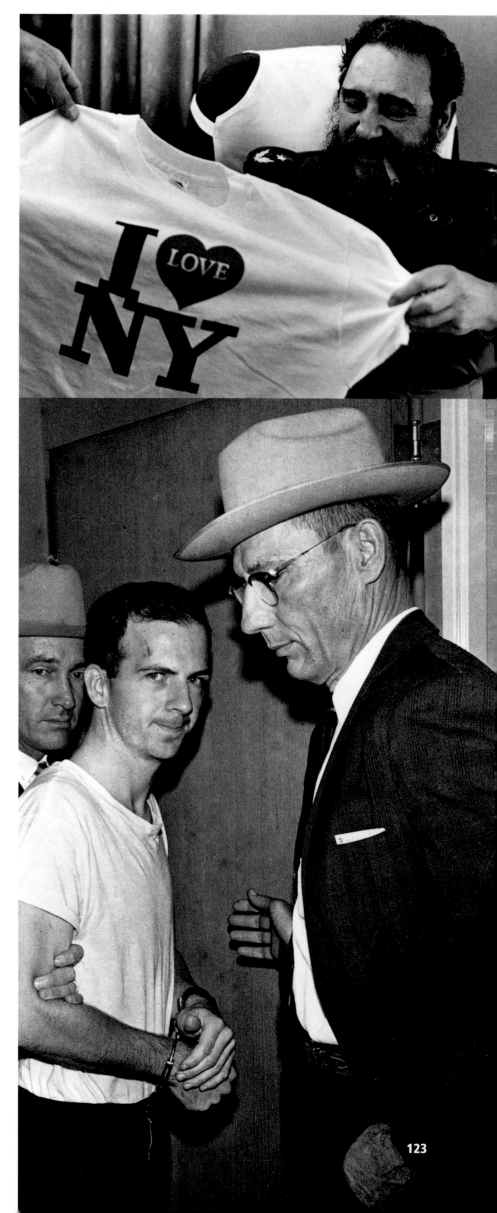

Not unlike an altarpiece in its totemic gravity, themes of racism, homophobia, AIDS, and sexuality are introduced in this tableau called *Fear*. From the series *Death Hope Fear* by British artists Gilbert and George, 1984.

Above: National Guardsmen kill four students at Kent State University in Ohio, and Vietnam spills into the streets of America. 1970.
Below: On the 50th aniversary of suffrage, the women's liberation movement links arms for equality on Fifth Avenue.
Photograph by Russell Reif, New York, 1970.

Stepchild of the radical movements of the 60s,
the revolution in lesbian and gay culture exploded in the 70s.
Photograph by Ronald Wood, 1971.

Left to right, top to bottom: As American as Independence Day, even presidents are found wearing the T: Jimmy Carter, Harry S Truman, Ronald Reagan, Franklin D. Roosevelt, and John F. Kennedy.

San Salvador. Photograph by Harry Mattison, 1980.

Bosnia. Photograph by Sebastiao Salgado, 1994.

132   **Above:** The T-shirt cozies up. *Domestic Scene, Broadchalke, Wilts.* Painting by David Hockney, 1963.
Below: The T in plein-air. *Two Figures.* Collage by Alex Katz, 1955.

Autumn Leaves

At 66 just learning how to take care of my body
to wake cheerful 8 AM & write in a notebook
rising from bed side naked leaving a naked boy asleep by the wall
mix miso mushroom leeks & winter squash breakfast,
Check bloodsugar, clean teeth exactly, brush, toothpick, floss,
    mouthwash
oil my feet, put on white shirt white pants white sox
sit solitary by the sink
a moment before brushing my hair, happy not yet
to be a corpse.

    – Allen Ginsberg

The Beat Goes On: a mock battle between two legendary writers. William Burroughs vs. Jack Kerouac.
Photograph by Allen Ginsberg, 1953.

Left: Drawing by Richard Giglio, 1986.
Below, top: Picasso in his studio at La Villa Californie, France. Photograph by Lee Miller, 1956.
Below, bottom: "Enfant terrible" Truman Capote, feral among the fronds in Key West. Photograph by Henri-Cartier-Bresson, 1946.

I asked Kenny to tell me about Ellen Marks, the former graduate student from Indiana University who was brutally murdered one night a few years ago. She was living in a shack on Pigeon Hill. Ellen was mutilated and decapitated; her severed head was never recovered. As Kenny spoke he gummed a piece of venison that his toothless mouth struggled to chew. He loved Ellen, he told me. When she was killed he was beside himself with grief. He even made a life-size robot to help the FBI flush out the murderer. It could walk and talk. It knew right from wrong, he told me. It knew God. It was jealous of other women and would wrap its sinewy arms around Kenny when he came home. Would I like to see it? In a minute he stormed downstairs with a six foot tall urethane foam construction that looked amazingly life-like. It was fully clothed and had brown hair that Kenny's sister Aola crocheted. Using tiny scissors Kenny had painstakingly sculpted a face into which he inserted his own false teeth. In the apartment redolent of deer meat, cockroaches raced up and down the walls while Kenny talked. He called the robot Brook. Why, I ask? For the babbling brook sound Ellen always made when she giggled. Besides he added h...

couldn't stand to call it Ellen all the time. In fact, he usually referred to it as "Tauquanah" which is Sioux for "Little Fox." Kenny was part Sioux, Cherokee and Cajun. And he and Ellen were married according to a Sioux custom whereby if a woman enters a teepee in which a single man is present, they are considered as man and wife. As we talked a woman rushed into the apartment. She desperately needed a witness for her wedding: she was to be married at 5:30. It's 4:00 now. No volunteers so she scurried back outside. The roar of cars hot-rodding up and down the street rattled the room. Aola is off in a corner chain smoking unfiltered Camels and munching chocolate-covered marshmallow cookies. Rays of sunlight pierced the room's smoky interior in straight lines. Aola was studying for her Graduate Equivalency Diploma. She's surprised the cops didn't send up Buck Flick, her ex-husband who'd already done time for murder— pushed an old man down a flight of steps during an argument. Instead a drifter named Robert E. Lee, Jr. was tried and convicted of first degree murder in the death of Ellen Marks. Kenny and Aola agreed that, in any case, Lee did not act alone. The conversation took a turn toward Satanic ritual as a possible motive for the crime. A few weeks later I run into Aola's husband, Augie, at Ace Pawn Shop. He is trying to pawn some old tools to raise cash to fix his van. Kenny, he tells me, died last night of a massive heart attack. They found him in his bed already expired. He never had a chance. Aola is really broken up.

136 **Above:** A love story between Kenny and a woman (whose death mask he carries) killed in a Bloomington, Indiana, housing project where they both lived. Murder on Pigeon Hill. Photograph by Jeffrey Wolin, 1991.
Right: Conceptual artist John Baldessari puts himself in the picture. *I Don't Need This . . . Quadruple Portrait.* Photographs with mixed media. 1995.

138 **Above:** Willem de Kooning contemplates pure lines, distilled form in his studio in East Hampton, New York. Photograph by Duane Michals, 1985.
Right: PAJAMA: PAul Cadmus and JAred French, photograph by MArgaret French, three collaborative artists known for stylized tableaux.
Fire Island, New York, 1945.

Bibliography

Books

Ash, Juliet, and Elizabeth Wilson. **Chic Thrills, A Fashion Reader**. Berkeley: University of California Press, 1993.

Ash, Juliet, and Lee Wright, eds. **Components of Dress: Design, Manufacturing and Image-Making in the Fashion Industry**. London and New York: Routledge, 1988.

Baker, Patricia. **Fashions of a Decade. The 1940s**. New York: Facts on File,1992.

Banta, Martha. **Imaging American Women: Idea and Ideals in Cultural History**. New York: Columbia University Press, 1987.

Barthes, Roland. **Système de la mode**. Paris: Éditions du Seuil, 1967.

Benstock, Shari, and Suzanne Ferriss. **On Fashion**. New Brunswick, N. J.: Rutgers University Press, 1994.

Brain, Robert. **The Decorated Body**. London: Hutchinson and Co., 1979.

Breward, Christopher. **The Culture of Fashion**. Manchester, England: Manchester University Press, 1995.

Carlyle, Thomas. **Sartor Resartus**. In **The Works of Thomas Carlyle**. London, 1896-99.

Carnegy, Vicki. **Fashions of a Decade. The 1980s**. New York: Facts on File,1990.

Carter, Alison. **Underwear: The Fashion History**. New York: Drama Book Publishers, 1992.

Chambers, Ian. **Popular Culture, The Metropolitan Experience**. London: Methuen, 1986.

Chenoune, Farid. **A History of Men's Fashion**. Paris: Flammarion, 1993.

Connikie, Yvonne. **Fashions of a Decade. The 1960s**. New York: Facts on File, 1990.

Cunnington, Phillis, and C. Willett. **The History of Underclothes**. New York: Dover Publications, Inc., 1992.

Davis, Fred. **Fashion, Culture and Identity**. Chicago: University of Chicago Press, 1992.

Dutton, Kenneth R. **The Perfectible Body. The Western Ideal of Male Physical Development**. New York: Continuum, 1995.

Ebin, Victoria. **The Body Decorated**. London: Thames and Hudson, 1979.

Engelmeier, Peter, and Regine Engelmeier. **Fashion in Film**. Munich: Prestel-Verlag, 1990.

Fausch, Deborah. **Architecture: In Fashion**. New York: Princeton Architectural Press, 1994.

Feldman, Elaine. **Fashions of a Decade. The 1990s**. New York: Facts on File, 1992.

Flugel, J.C. **The Psychology of Clothes**. London: The Hogarth Press, Ltd., 1950.

Fresener, Scott. **The T-shirt Book**. Salt Lake City: Gibbs-Smith, 1995.

Glynn, Prudence. **In Fashion: Dress in the Twentieth Century**. New York: Oxford University Press, 1978.

————. **Skin to Skin: Eroticism in Dress**. New York: Oxford University Press, 1982.

Grattaroti, Rosalie. **Great T-shirt Graphics**. Rockport: Rockport Publishers, 1993.

Herald, Jacqueline. **Fashions of a Decade. The 1970s**. New York: Facts on File, 1992.

Hollander, Anne. **Seeing through Clothes**. New York: Viking Press, 1978.

————. **Sex and Suits**. New York: Knopf, 1994.

Horn, Marilyn, and Lois M. Gurel. **The Second Skin**. Boston: Houghton Mifflin Company, 1981.

Kidwell, Claudia, and Margaret C. Christman. **Suiting Everyone**. Washington, D.C.: Smithsonian Institution Press, 1974.

Kidwell, Claudia, and Valerie Steele. **Men and Women: Dressing the Part**. Washington, D.C.: Smithsonian Institution Press, 1989.

Laver, James. **Costume & Fashion**. London: Thames and Hudson, 1995.

Lewenhaupt, Tony, and Claës Leuwenhaupt. **Crosscurrents: Art, Fashion, Design, 1890-1989**. New York: Rizzoli International Publications, Inc., 1989.

Ley, Sandra. **Fashion for Everyone: The Story of Ready-to-Wear, 1870-1970**. New York: Scribner, 1970.

McDowell, Colin. **Dressed to Kill: Sex, Power & Clothes**. London: Hutchinson and Co., 1992.

Martin, Richard, and Harold Koda. **Jocks and Nerds: Men's Style in the Twentieth Century**. New York: Rizzoli International Publications, Inc., 1989.

Mollo, John. **Military Fashion**. New York: Macmillan, 1978.

Polhemus, Ted. **Streetstyle: From Sidewalk to Catwalk**. London: Thames and Hudson, 1994.

————, and Lynn Procter. **Fashion and Anti-fashion**. London: Thames and Hudson, 1978.

Ribeiro, Aileen. **Dress and Morality**. London: Batsford, 1986.

Riesman, David. **The Lonely Crowd**. New Haven: Yale University Press, 1961.

Rubinstein, Ruth P. **Dress Codes, Meanings, and Messages in American Culture**. Boulder, Colorado: Westview Press, 1995.

Schoeffler, O. E., and William Gale. **Esquire's Encyclopedia of 20th Century Men's Fashions**. New York: McGraw-Hill, 1973.

Sichel, Marion. **Vol. 9** of **Costume Reference. 1939-1950**. London: Batsford, 1987.

Squire, Geoffrey. **Dress, Art, and Society**. London: Studio Vista, 1974.

Steele, Valerie. **Fashion and Eroticism**. New York: Oxford University Press, 1985.

Periodicals

Beller, Thomas. "The Problem with T-shirts." **The New Yorker**, May 3, 1993, p. 35.

Berne, Betsy. "Street Talk." **Vogue**, April 1996, p. 122.

Betts, Katherine. "Men's Tanks." **Vogue**, April 1992, p. 208.

————. "Tee Time." **Vogue**, February 1994, p. 81.

Bloomfield, Judy. "T-shirts: Back to the Sixties." **Women's Wear Daily**, September 28, 1988, p. 6.

Brown, David. "Mosh and War: Even after 20-odd Years...." **Entertainment Weekly**, August 25, 1995, p. 108.

Chunn, Louise. "Fashion's Conscience." **British Vogue**, December 1995, p. 142.

Deitz, Paula. "The Undershirt Comes Out." **The New York Times Magazine/Fashions of The Times**, Spring 1994, p. 56-58.

DuCann, Charlotte. "The Legend of Protest." **New Statesman & Society**, May 19, 1989, p. 12.

Feder, Carol. "T-shirts: Bona Fide Fashion." **Stores**, January 1991, p. 71.

Gardner, Marilyn. "T-shirt Designs Spell... Messages." **The Christian Science Monitor**, October 13, 1992, p. 13.

Giovannini, Marco. "E la T-shirt si veste di arte." **Per Lui**, May 1984, p. 158-63.

Goldbergs, Michael. "Rock's New Gift of Garb." **Rolling Stone**, November 3, 1988, p. 15.

Grimes, William. "West 57th: A T-shirt for Every Theme." **The New York Times**, November 24, 1995, p. C1.

Hu, Holly. "Clothed in Truth." **New Statesman & Society**, October 4, 1991, p. 17.

Kopkind, Andrew. "From A to Tee." **Harper's Bazaar**, July 1993, p. 31.

Martin, Richard. "VOTE: The 92 Election." **Textile and Text 14,** 1992, p. 30.

————, and Harold Koda. "T-Line: Expressions of Our Time in the T-shirts...." **Textile and Text 14**, 1991, p. 13-21.

Monget, Karyn. "Underwear's Power Pair." **Women's Wear Daily**, February 6, 1995, p. 3.

Nelton, Sharon. "The Man Who Transformed T-shirts...." **Nation's Business**, January 1991, p. 11.

Nieves, Evelyn. "T-shirts Can Broadcast Civilized Messages, Too." **The New York Times**, November 16, 1993, pp. A18 and B6.

Phalon, Richard. "Fashion for Peace." **Spin**, April 1991, pp. 7, 60-71.

————. "Walking Billboards." **Forbes**, December 7, 1992, p. 81.

Reed, J.D. "Hail to the T, the Shirt That Speaks Volumes." **Smithsonian**, April 1992, p. 96.

Romero, Michele. "Happy Days Are Here Again." **Entertainment Weekly**, August 26, 1994, p. 20.

Swanbrow, Diane. "Talking T-shirts: America's Raunchy New Ritual." **Human Behavior,** March 1979, p. 12.

Van Gelder, Lindsey. "The Little White Shirt." **Allure**, June 1992, p. 90.

Van Meter, Jonathan. "Fast Fashion." **Vogue**, June 1990, p. 258-59.

Credits

cover / back cover
Courtesy Harry Benson.

endpapers
Courtesy Cornell Capa, Magnum Photos.

endpapers
Raymond Depardon, Magnum Photos.

page 2
Courtesy Herb Ritts.

page 6
The National Archives.

page 7
Courtesy Bruce Davidson, Magnum Photos.

page 8
Courtesy John Engstead, Warner Brothers,
The Kobal Collection.

page 9
Courtesy Ralph Gibson.

page 10
Courtesy Arthur Elgort.

page 11
Courtesy Eric Fischl, Mary Boone Gallery, New
York. Jerry Speyer Family Collection, New York.
108 x 78 inches, oil on canvas.

page 12
Courtesy Albert Watson.

page 14
Courtesy the U.S. Navy.

page 16-17
Courtesy The Jimmy Allen Collection.

page 18
Courtesy Mississippi Department of Archives
and History. Courtesy U.S. Navy.

page 23
Courtesy U.S. Navy.

page 24-25
Courtesy U.S. Army.

page 26
Eliot Elisofon, *Life* Magazine ©Time Inc.,
reprinted by permission.

page 27
U.S. Navy, FPG, International Corp.

page 28
Courtesy U.S. Army; UPI/Bettmann.

page 29
UPI/Bettmann.

page 30
The Bettmann Archive.

page 31
Los Alamos National Archives.

page 32
Courtesy Sebastiao Salgado.

page 34-35
The Bettmann Archive.

page 36
Courtesy Howard Greenberg Gallery.

page 37
Weegee, ©1994, The International Center of
Photography, New York, the bequest of Wilma Wilcox.

page 38
Courtesy Steven Klein.

page 39
Courtesy Jill Freedman.

page 40-41
Courtesy Mitch Epstein.

page 43
The Bettmann Archive.

page 44-45
Courtesy Joseph Rodriguez.

page 4
Dorothea Lange, The Library of Congress.

page 47
Courtesy Morris Engel, Howard Greenberg Gallery.

page 48
Courtesy the Aperture Foundation,
The Paul Strand Archive.

page 49
Courtesy Chantal Regnault.

page 50
Courtesy Leon Levinstein, Howard Greenberg Gallery.

page 51
Courtesy Arthur Tress.

page 52-53
Courtesy Bruce Davidson, Magnum Photos.

page 54-55
Courtesy Estate of Garry Winogrand,
Fraenkel Gallery, San Francisco.

page 56
Courtesy Lynn Goldsmith, LGI Photo Agency.

page 58
Courtesy Photofest; Courtesy Joshua Greene,
©1994 Archive of Milton H. Greene; Courtesy The
Everett Collection; United Artists, Courtesy The Kobal
Collection; Courtesy Neal Peters Collection.

page 59
Warner Brothers, Courtesy The Kobal Collection;
Archive Pictures; Columbia Pictures, Courtesy
The Kobal Collection; Archive Pictures; FPG;
Archive Pictures.

page 60
Courtesy Annie Leibovitz.

page 61
Courtesy Albert Watson.

page 64
Courtesy Herb Ritts.

page 65
Courtesy Philip Dixon.

page 66
Courtesy Neal Peters Collection.

page 67
Phil Stern; Courtesy Photofest; Courtesy Neal Peters
Collection; Courtesy The Kobal Collection.

page 68
Courtesy Herman Leonard,
Catherine Edelman Gallery, Chicago.

page 69
Courtesy Burt Glinn, Magnum Photos.

page 70
Courtesy Albert Watson.

page 71
Courtesy Herb Ritts.

page 72
Courtesy Matthew Rolston, Fahey/Klein Gallery,
Los Angeles.

page 73
Courtesy Matthew Rolston, Fahey/Klein Gallery,
Los Angeles.

page 74
Courtesy Lynn Goldsmith, LGI Photo Agency.

page 75
Courtesy Greg Gorman; Courtesy Adrian Boot,
Retna Ltd.

page 76
Courtesy Annie Leibovitz.

page 77
Courtesy Neal Peters Collection.

page 78
Courtesy Herb Ritts.

page 79
Courtesy Greg Gorman.

page 80
Courtesy Arthur Tress.

page 82
Courtesy Guzman.

page 83
Paramount, Courtesy The Kobal Collection.

page 84
Courtesy The Alberto Vargas Estate. Vargas is a
registered trademark of The Vargas Partnership.

page 85
Estate of Robert Doisneau, Rapho Agency.

page 86
Courtesy Gianni Versace.

page 87
Courtesy The Tom of Finland Foundation, Los Angeles.

page 88
Courtesy D.C. Moore Gallery, New York.
Courtesy Duane Michals.

page 89
Courtesy George Platt Lynes, II, D.C. Moore Gallery,
New York.

page 90
Courtesy Andrea Blanch, Jed Root Inc.

page 91
Courtesy Nan Goldin.

page 92-93
Courtesy Michael Halsband.

page 94
Courtesy John Gutmann, Fraenkel Gallery,
San Francisco; The Bettmann Archive.

page 95
Courtesy Association des Amis de Jacques-Henri
Lartigue, Paris; Courtesy William Klein, Howard
Greenberg Gallery.

page 96
Courtesy Annie Leibovitz.

page 97
Sabine Weiss, Rapho Agency.

page 98
Hy Peskin, *Sports Illustrated*.

page 99
Estate of Robert Riger, The James Danziger Gallery,
New York.

page 100-101
Courtesy Jane Corkin Gallery, Toronto.
©Margaret Bourke White.

page 102
Courtesy Michael Thompson, Jed Root Inc.

page 104
Courtesy Association des Amis de Jacques-Henri
Lartigue, Paris.

page 105
Courtesy Jockey International, Inc.

page 107
Courtesy Corinne Day, *Vogue,* ©Conde Nast
Publications.

page 109
Courtesy Steven Meisel.

page 110
Courtesy Peter Lindbergh.

page 111
Courtesy Gianni Versace.

page 112
Courtesy Matthew Rolston, Fahey/Klein Gallery,
Los Angeles.

page 113
Courtesy Peter Lindbergh.

page 114
Courtesy Didier Malige.

page 115
Courtesy Patrick Demarchelier.

page 116-117
Courtesy Christian Witkin.

page 118-119
©Estate of Brian Weil, from every 17 seconds,
Aperture, New York, 1992.

page 120
Black Star.

page 121
Rick Friedman, Black Star.

page 122
Karen Ranucci, Black Star; The Bettmann Archive.

page 124-125
Courtesy Gilbert and George,
Anthony d'Offay Gallery, London.

page 126
Black Star; Russell Reif, Black Star.

page 127
Ronald Wood, Black Star.

page 128-129
FPG International Corp.; Bettmann Archive;
Courtesy JFK Library, Ronald Reagan Library, FDR
Library and Harry S Truman Library.

page 130
Courtesy Harry Mattison.

page 131
Courtesy Sebastiao Salgado.

page 132
Courtesy David Hockney; Courtesy Alex Katz,
Robert Miller Gallery, New York.

page 133
Courtesy Allen Ginsberg.

page 134
Courtesy Richard Giglio.

page 135
Courtesy The Lee Miller Archives, England;
Henri Cartier-Bresson, Magnum Photos.

page 136
Courtesy Jeffrey Wolin,
Catherine Edelman Gallery, Chicago.

page 137
Courtesy John Baldessari.

page 138
Courtesy Duane Michals.

page 139
Courtesy D.C. Moore Gallery, New York.

page 140
Courtesy Richter, *The New Yorker* Magazine, Inc.

Page 143
Courtesy Annie Leibovitz.

page 144
Courtesy Larry Burrows, Laurence Miller Gallery,
New York. *Life* Magazine ©Time Inc., reprinted by
permission.

endpapers
FPG International Corp.

Grateful thanks to the artists, agencies, and galleries who graciously donated their reproduction fees for this project, noted above by the prefix "Courtesy . . . ."
Poster films donated by PPI and Gordon and Raoul Goff.

Acknowledgments

To the geniuses—Catherine Chermayeff, Nan Richardson, and Bill Anton—you made my vision a reality.

To Giorgio Armani—thank you for your eloquent introduction.

Mom and Dad—I love you—and to Gigi and Harry Benson, Marcie Bloom, Dan Galpern, Margaret Jaworski, Felicia Jones, Barbara Manocherian, Julie Saul, Donna Summer Sudano and Bruce Sudano, Lorraine Toto, and Peter Tunney— I thank you for being incredible friends!

—Alice Harris

Our grateful thanks go to the following for their generous assistance, advice, and information:
Joseph Montebello for life-giving enthusiasm and unstinting professionalism.

Miles Barth, ICP; Dr. Walter Bradford, U.S. Army Center of Military History; Robert Brewer and Roger Meade, Los Alamos National Laboratory Archives; Ron Brewster at the Pink Palace Museum, Memphis; Dawn Brown, Isaac Mizrahi; Kelly Carroon, Maggie Gross, Hilary Rush, Linda Sterling, The Gap; Anne Christensen; Courtenay Clinton; Grace Coddington; Jane Corkin; Jeanne Courtmanche, Aperture; Quentin Crisp; Kate de Castelbajac; Grace Darby, The New Yorker; Jonathan David; Gerald Dearing; Edward DeLuca, D.C. Moore Gallery; Faisal Devji; Stephen Dubner; Leslie Dunton-Downer; Catherine Edelman; Mary Engel, Ruth Orkin Archive; Patricia Everett; David Fahey, Fahey/Klein Gallery; Masood Farivar; Dennis Favello, Edward Fergal, U.S. Navy Museum; Andrea Ferronato; Ellen Shanley and Fred Dennis, F.I.T.; Linda Gaunt, Giorgio Armani; Allen Ginsberg; Julie Graham, Retna Ltd; Joshua Greene, Milton Greene Archive; Peter Hale; Vicki Harris, Laurence Miller Gallery; Lizzie Himmel; Pat Hodo and Blanchard Sherry, Department of Southern Culture, University of Mississippi, Oxford; Aaron Hamburger, Fraenkel Gallery; Valentine Hooven, Tom of Finland Foundation; Lauren Hutton; Andy Karsch; Claudia Brush Kidwell, Smithsonian; David Kuhn; Lady Bunny; Paul Ludick; Ron Maglioso and Josh Siegal, MOMA, New York; Rob Magnotta, Edge Agency; Michael Mailer; Didier Malige; Fern Mallis, CFDA; Mary Jane Marcasiano; Greil Marcus; Richard Martin at the Costume Institute of the Metropolitan Museum of Art; Raul Martinez; Michael McNamara and Ira Livingston, Cotton, Inc; Steven Mnuchin; Kim Kassel Mnuchin and Jenia Molnar, Calvin Klein; Anthony Montoya, Paul Strand Archive; Felix de N'Yourt; Leah Nicole; Kelly Steis, Susan Kowal, Kate Egnatz, and especially Raoul and Gordon Goff, Palace Press; Neal Peters; George Platt Lynes, II; Josephine Pryde, Anthony d'Offay Gallery, London; Craig Reynolds; Michael Reynolds; Yancey Richardson; Brad Robb at the Cotton Board; Jeff Rosenheim, Metropolitan Museum of Art; Bob Rosenthal; Diana Ross; Mark Royce; Kathy Ryan; Charlotte Schapiro, Jockey International; Barbara Schlager; Arnold Schwarzenegger; Steve Shore; Leslie Simitch; Carrie Springer, Howard Greenberg Gallery; Bruce Springsteen; Pam Stein, KCD; David Strettel; Cavett Taff of the Mississippi Department of Archives and History; Tina Thor; John Travolta; John Van Eck, Cottonlandia, Greenwood, Mississippi; Astrid Vargas-Conte; Gianni Versace; Neville Wakefield; Ron Warren, Mary Boone Gallery; Megan Wilson; Tim Wright, LGI Agency; Nancy Young, Hanes.

The following individuals and companies generously donated T-shirts for the jacket poster:
Sharon Bailey; Patti Blau, Nonsense, Miami, Fl.; Chris Campagnola; Ivan Chermayeff; Sam Chermayeff; Jonathan David; Loulou and Fanny David; Sarah Dent at Crunch; GMHC; Samantha Harris; Tommy Hilfiger; Yung Jo; Calvin Klein; Rhonda Lindle; Marco, Marcoart, 186 Orchard Street, NYC 10002; Paul Marti, Haight-Asbury T-Shirts, 1500 Haight St., San Francisco, Ca. 94117, 1-800-851-7364; Pablo Miraballes; Kathy McCarver Mnuchin; Oilily; Laura Whitcomb at Label.

—Umbra Editions

Cover Models: Marie Elena Marino and Bruce Messite

Uniformity meets conformity at a Tokyo driving range. Photograph by Larry Burrows, 1964.

Effervescent energy, sunset and beach balls. Cannes, France, circa 1930.